Pretty WEiRD

Overcoming Impostor Syndrome and Other Oddly Empowering Lessons

Marissa Miller

Skyhorse Publishing

TABLE OF CONTENTS

To Mom, Dad, Michelle and Bubby: this one's for you.

INTRODUCTION

Growing up without a Designated Cool Female to guide me through the rituals of womanhood, I became that kid in second grade making my Barbie dolls reenact Kama Sutra positions and storing things in my nose to "see what would happen" (spoiler: that sequin from my friend Sammy's shoe was never to be seen again). It was no secret that I was different. But to feel like I was in on the joke, I called myself a weirdo in an essay on my love of death metal in the school newspaper. It was the closest thing to writing for *Cosmopolitan* I could get at age thirteen, and the closest I could get to controlling my own narrative far before I knew what that word meant.

Magazines were always my Sherpa up the hill we'll call puberty, thin lines and sharp edges my only real example of who to be when I had no idea which step came next in girlhood after exhausting every Spice Girls choreography, my breasts bouncing along timidly as they grew in at different speeds. I couldn't tell what came first: that my hatred of my growing body led me to magazines, or that magazines led me to hate my body. Given that my earliest memory includes walking back from day camp at three years old and throwing a tantrum because my inner thighs were touching, let's go with the former.

I didn't look, feel, or act anything like the images of people in the magazines or the authors who profiled them. But it's not like I publicly aspired to be anything like them. Gosh, no. Middle-of-the-road suburban kids like me were doomed for mediocre lives full of A-line skirts and single glasses of white wine at stuffy networking events. Mediocrity was something I had come to accept and even embrace—until everything changed my last two years of high school. I was winning national poetry and public speaking competitions; I was being profiled in newsletters for my budding writing career; and teachers paraded my work as prime examples of how to write as part of their class syllabi. And yet, nothing about me became any more glamorous. I was still the kid with an inability to keep her bowel schedule to herself. I was still explaining to boyfriends' parents for the first time upon meeting them that lycopene, an antioxidant found in tomatoes and watermelon, has been proven to have anticancerous properties on both the prostate and uterus. For the first time, my magazines fell short in showing me how to live, what to look like, and what to do with my life.

There was literally no way of reconciling those two diametrically opposing facets of my identity—the freak and the ambitious student—without diving headfirst into an existential crisis. By that point, I had assumed psychiatric medication was strictly reserved for folks who had imaginary friends and that therapy was something old married couples did, so I figured there was no point Going There unless I had a backup coping mechanism.

I was finally able to give my general feelings of malaise a concrete name when I first heard the term "impostor syndrome" during my last year of high school, around the time when my grades and academic performance started to be decent enough not to make me sweat through my thick uniform when I got my report card in a manilla envelope at the end of the school day four times a year. A Google search of all my symptoms like "Can't take credit for any of my success," "This is all an accident," and "Don't feel like I deserve all these good things" led me to case studies about other women experiencing the same things. Most of them were high-powered CEOs who felt completely inadequate despite evidence of the contrary. Others possessed inborn exquisite talents that catapulted them to a level of fame they believed was unwarranted. All I had to show for my success was a bunch of stints on the honor roll and some dollar store-purchased awards on my wall for writing angsty MySpace poems, which I then submitted to contests because the only accounts to interact with my content were porn bots. So, not only did I have no real place in the high school cafeteria but I also had no place in the impostor syndrome sufferers' high-powered corner office league either. Feeling like a fraudulent impostor was a complicated feeling no Google rabbit hole—and apparently no back issue of *Cosmo*—would ever be able to fix.

It turns out examining and reflecting on my own life, instead of looking externally, was just the thing my high school guidance counselor didn't order—but should have.

I don't want to ruin it for you because I spent a painstaking amount of time outlining in profane, vivid detail what exactly I reflected on. But hopefully, you'll walk away from this little piece of literature understanding that our feelings of inadequacy often mean we deserve all those great things that happen to us. We're worthy of success by virtue of us thinking we're not. Unlike folks who expect standing ovations for simply existing (*cough* finance bros *cough*), us impostors constantly strive to do better and be better in order to avoid being outed as frauds. The people splayed on magazine centerfolds you dream of emulating think they're hella weird, too. And if they don't? Well, you don't have much in common with them anyway, and you really don't want to sit through happy hour with someone like that.

But don't worry. We probably have lots in common. In this essay collection, you'll learn that I wasn't always this enlightened. Going to therapy would have been a big middle finger to my parents for giving me—on paper—what I thought was a fairly solid suburban upbringing. Instead, my sadness became a covert operation, taking on an almost tangible, human-like quality with its persistence and level of intensity growing by day. My sadness was the pre-rolled joints in my purse hidden in tubes of lipstick. My sadness was the rubber band I snapped against my inner wrist to distract myself from hunger. My sadness was a string of sexual assaults that I counted as standard teenage promiscuity.

No matter how many times I flirted with the idea of sawing off my love handles with an axe or how many hours I spent with an electric toothbrush down my throat after Rosh Hashanah dinner (I was never successful), I felt that as a white woman from an upstanding nuclear family with a roof over my head and food on the table, I had no right to seek help or support for my feelings of inferiority. Sadness wasn't allowed to happen to people like me. I, like so many, reside in that liminal space of being too normal to stand out, yet too weird to fit in.

I expected my sadness to subside once I started meeting all the widely agreed-upon criteria of success: I became a small business owner leading a freelance journalism career writing for the likes of the *New York Times*, the *Washington Post*, *Wall Street Journal*, *Vogue*, *GQ*, CNN, and *Cosmopolitan*. I taught journalism workshops, and I was invited to speak on panels, on the radio, and at schools around my hometown of Montreal. College students did projects on my career that earned them actual grades. Writing service journalism for the publications I grew up idolizing became my way of guiding others through their lives, but secretly, like many of us, I had very little clue how to live my own. I'm not a "writer," I thought. I'm just some unhygienic cat lady with illegal access to Microsoft Office.

The transition away from the "weird" one to the "successful" one felt like a performative Halloween costume that didn't quite fit. It left me with questions like, "How are women supposed to own their achievements if we've been told from the beginning to stay quiet?" "How are we supposed to strive for greater things when pride is narcissism's low-brow cousin?" "How are we supposed to feel like we deserve our successes—big and small—if social media etiquette dictates we're overcompensating for something bigger when we post about our professional victories, our growing families, and our newfound mastery of That Cool New Yoga Pose That'll Allow You to Lick Your Own Lady Parts?" "Why have we regressed into an archaic Dark Age where those who keep quiet about their accomplishments on social media—or better yet, leave no digital footprint—are of the superior race?"

Here's a Hot Take: a significant chunk of Beyoncé's allure lies in having not posted anything on Instagram for years after creating her account. We conjured truths about her in our own minds with the same fury we used to dissect her pregnancy announcement and cardiovascularly demanding Coachella performance alongside sister Solange. The less we say about ourselves, the more room there is for people to draw their own (sometimes positive) conclusions about us, because we don't give them the opportunity to think otherwise. My job is to literally say things all the time, and with that, I invite a special brand of criticism only a 9:00 a.m. shot of Jameson can fix.

My mom and dad—second- and third-generation Canadians who fought for their place in the workforce and feel as though they damn well earned it—don't understand my identity crisis–driven plight *Enters stage right wearing Avril Lavigne Purim costume*. They see us all as entitled millennials who operate under the assumption that it's our God-given right to succeed and that we can't buy real estate because we've maxed out our credit cards on Jeffree Star eyeshadow palettes. They're not wrong. We cover up our perceived shortcomings with Instagram posts that strategically crop out unmade beds and tears, self-congratulatory Facebook proclamations and eyebrows that took so long to perfect we were there to witness the first sprout of gray hair like a tulip in spring. I wish I could turn to my peers for support, for validation, so they could tell me that I earned my achievements—that I am Good at Being Me. But instead I'm turning inward because they're sick of my shit. And, again, my psychiatrist didn't think of prescribing it even though he knows my selective serotonin reuptake inhibitors haven't been working properly for the last six years.

My loneliness wouldn't have felt so pronounced if I knew others had been experiencing it, too. Forget wine— what really helps the antidepressants go down is the act of normalizing each other's anxiety-fueled inner-monologues. Most of your friends, family, colleagues, and idols all grapple with the same condition. I have nothing to lose by talking about it. Except for maybe a few of my more vanilla acquaintances who've had it UP TO HERE with my potty mouth.

Chapter 1
PELVIC FLOORED

My left ribcage felt hard and cold on the linoleum floor. I read once in a women's magazine with Jennifer Aniston on the cover that lying on your left side reduces pain. Women's magazines are my rulebook, my dogma, my Sherpa up the hill when I am lost. I am always lost. My inner Siri is rarely activated.

"There is a scissor cutting its way through my insides and it won't stop," I told Noah, my boyfriend at the time, between hasty rhythmic breaths. "I feel it moving and it's running around. I change my mind. It's not scissors, it's a dagger."

He could tell, for once, that I was not being a neurotic princess.

The gluten-free pasta on the stove above me hardened around the sides of the metal pot. He rubbed my lower belly, each stroke an invitation to relax and find my "Zen" like the magazines promised.

"I'm begging you to just take a bite out of something. Please. I'm begging you," he said, kneeling down on the floor beside me. "You need the energy for tomorrow. I don't want to see another situation where I almost have to take you to the emergency room like that time you fucking passed out on the streets of Manhattan."

I was now crouched on my kitchen floor with my head between my knees, just like I was six months before in 2015 on the sidewalk of 3rd Avenue and East 67th Street. It was late May, and I had just wrapped up a meeting with my editor at *Cosmopolitan*. I sauntered out of the Hearst building with the weightlessness of a tumbleweed down a dirt road.

I refused to eat before our meeting so as to not clog my thoughts with diner omelette grease. I always think better when I don't eat, or so I think. When I left the Hearst building, I was running on the high of fair-trade iced coffee and a new story assignment, until cataracts—or what felt like them—clouded my eyes. My knees buckled, sending me to the ground. Noah pulled me up by the cold, damp wrist and dragged me into a nearby pizzeria.

"Quick, please, my girlfriend is fainting. She needs water now," he'd pled into a crowded ether the year before. He sat me down onto a chair like a ventriloquist, propping my head up with his calloused hands. I felt the sweat droplets descend down each vertebrae of my spine, the cold chair against my tailbone. I belonged on the sidewalk, free from the confines of food and chairs and restaurants and calories and people who told me what to do.

Back on my linoleum kitchen floor, I knew I couldn't pull that same shit.

"I'm begging you to just take a bite out of something. Please," he continued. The desperation in his eyes the texture and color of a mahogany leather sofa pained me more than the emptiness did. "We have a post-marathon brunch we need to make it to. You need to get to that finish line."

Everything was about food. Food this. Food that. Couldn't I turn my body into a microcosmic cashless society where taking a bite of pasta doesn't feel like a life or death decision?

Noah was always right but that didn't say much because everyone is always a little more right than me, no matter how objectively right I am. The more he begged me to eat a spoonful of pasta hardening on the stove, the more it reinforced the idea that I really was doing it. This was thrilling. I was saying no to food again, just like I had done so well when I was fourteen years old. If I was going to think about how that one bite would affect me for the next twenty-four hours, I might as well eschew it altogether. But now, I wasn't some kid posting "Stay strong!!" on pro-anorexia blogs. I had an alibi. I was in excruciating physical pain.

"I can't do it. I will throw up and die," I told him, pleading for something I wasn't sure was even feasible. I

3

imagined the words sounding pitiful as they exited my quivering Blue-Man-Group lips, because that's what happens when you feel like a burden on people all the time. The pain was a pizza cutter soaring through my bodily diner grease.

I went to the bathroom to force out whatever monster made my body its home. I sat on the toilet with my head nesting in the palm of my hands and my shoulders hunched collapsing onto my lap. Nothing came out. Muscle spasms pinched my organs. Dead air whispered that I wasn't worthy of a working system. Whether that was digestive or reproductive, I didn't quite know.

I carefully peeled off my magenta Lululemon shorts and multiple sports bras I was wearing in anticipation for my half-marathon a meager four hours later (the key is to avoid clothes that chafe, unless you want to spend half the race jogging like a penguin with an inner thigh rash. I couldn't afford any more discomfort). I had too much pride to rub coconut oil—or worse, deodorant—between my gapless thighs.

The pain had morphed into what felt like a colony of bees zooming around my insides, liberally erecting their stingers to mark their territory. Even though I hadn't eaten anything in several hours, my stomach was now distended. There were boxing gloves mid-match in my abdomen, punching their way out. I was alone with my body. I was alone with the stabbing. Noah said some things about wanting to experience what I was feeling to make the pain go away.

I looked down to find a Hansel and Gretel trail of blood leading from my inner thighs down to my rough and flaky feet. Maraschino cherry-thick clumps stuck to my skin like leeches. Thick, red walls that should have been inside, it seemed, dangled like ornaments. What was more painful than the pain itself was the belief that I deserved it. My fingers were quivering too rapidly to Google what was happening to me, so I chalked it up to one of those horrifying periods women's magazines warn you about when you get an IUD.

A half an hour of sleep later, I was stepping into those same magenta shorts in preparation for the day's half-marathon.

* * *

I had an IUD inserted in 2012 because when you're a spacey adolennial (if the adolescent/millennial portmanteau actually takes off as a thing I will be very surprised), you don't trust yourself to take a birth control pill every day, let alone remember to turn off your hair straightening iron before you leave the house.

"Dr. Frontenac, on a scale from one to childbirth, how badly is this going to hurt?" I asked.

I was an open, spread-eagle wound with my feet in stirrups. But I was eager to finally rely on a method that's been touted both by women's service magazines and doctors alike to be fool- and fail-proof.

"I would give it a two," he said in a voice as shaky as his hands under condom-textured rubber gloves. His volume lowered considerably once I fastened on my journalist hat and started asking the Hard Questions, like will my boyfriend be able to feel the metal wire poking him when he's inside me; will I be able to rip it out with my own bare hands in a fit of rage; will airport security be able to pick it up on the metal detector; will this, like so many other things, make me feel sad and fat?

His answer to all of the above was a curt "No," as if I had asked a difficult multiple-choice question on a college entrance exam and when in doubt, always circle "C."

I never subscribed to the notion that all male gynecologists perceive their practice or their patients neutrally anyway. On a pathological level, there's something fascinating—terrifying even—about a heterosexual cisgender male who chooses to dedicate his livelihood toward treating an organ he will never fully understand no matter how many textbooks he reads. It's an organ that comes with a lot of emotional baggage: either multiple people attached to vaginas have rejected him, or he has derived so much satisfaction from a vagina that even the sight of a crying twenty-one-year-old patient bound to a gurney can't stop him from harkening back to that one time in his Camaro overlooking the sunset in 1987 with his first live-in girlfriend.

Dr. Frontenac was overcompensating. I imagined what sort of techniques he'd picked up in med school to optimize his bedside manner. I'm not sure where in the syllabus it suggested he ask me about my feelings toward the Palestinian-Israeli conflict while elbow-deep into my birth canal, but there we were. He poked around at my ovaries while looking at the ceiling like he was focusing on comparing grapefruit textures at the grocery store.

"Um, it's complicated, I guess?" I managed to squeeze out. "I mean, I have family in Israel so naturally I'm a little biased."

"On the count of three, I'm going to insert . . . " Dr. Frontenac trailed off.

If his language had been any more evocative of my mashed pumpkin-carrot "airplane zoom zoom" days as a baby, I'd have had to call airport security. I get that the countdown is intended to prepare the patient, but way to both infantilize and completely trigger me at the same time.

I buried my face in a series of panicked BlackBerry messages to my friend Liz. She's best described as a Greek goddess version of Aubrey Plaza with perfect eyebrows, every hair in place, and almond-shaped nails from those YouTube tutorials. Had I not known the intimate details of her digestive system, I would be too intimidated to talk to her in writing and reporting class. Liz had just bought a house with her fiancé, so I figured she wouldn't want to reenact their first vacation together in Cuba. After hitting up the resort buffet too hard, they engaged in an hour-long painful game of Battleshits. I mean, he proposed a day later, instilling hope in bloated women like me everywhere. Along with some crockpot-like device, I gave her potpourri marketed literally as "shit spray" for her bridal shower, which she opened in front of her entire Greek Orthodox family. She proceeded to read the instructions over the microphone. My cheeks turned rectal-polyp red. Had it just been Liz and I, the moment would have been perfect. Kind of like the digital moment I was having with her now.

Assuming cunnilingus position—my least favorite of them all—I felt very connected to Liz through my screen. I wasn't quite oozing liquid shit all over my gynecologist like she had on her betrothed, but it sure felt like I was about to. And she would be the only one to understand.

"its going in. 10/10 worst pain of my life freaking out help this pain is not even a little bit tolerable," I typed with haste.

The pressure of the IUD insertion made me light-headed as I sunk deeper into a lucid night terror. I was partially conscious, yet completely unable to control what happened next.

"Deep breaths babygirl u got this!!!" she typed with what I can only imagine were her signature baby pink almond-shaped acrylic nails tapping against tiny keys.

Her words were cooling, like the blue jelly sonographers slather across your stomach before an ultrasound. Specifically, the ultrasound that Dr. Frontenac would never end up using on me to detect the correct placement of said IUD.

I let out a guttural scream. I could no longer read the series of messages through what felt like the Niagara Falls streaming down my flushed cheeks. The IUD tore through my cervix and latched its claws onto my uterus. I could feel every millimeter of the procedure. In what world is that kind of pain a "two"?

With no more than a flash card reading the date of insertion (December 12, 2012, will forever be etched in my brain—and cervix), Dr. Frontenac shuffled me out the door to make room for the next passenger on his conveyer belt.

"Should be good for up to five years. Bye, bye, now," he said, waving me off like I had just held up the security line searching for my fucking passport again.

That wasn't a metaphor because I misplace it so often I'm convinced The Universe is beckoning me to stay in one place lest I do something stupid like ask for a birth control method that was, at that point, far more traumatizing an option than delivering and raising a child on a freelance journalist's salary.

I couldn't get up on his command. Had anyone walked in, they would have assumed I was the subject of an autopsy. Everything from my waist down felt numb, so I opened my eyes to ensure it was all there. I could see my pelvis. It was definitely there in the literal sense. But the area was a phantom limb. The only thing confirming my existence was blood.

* * *

It was the summer of 2010. I spent the weeks between my job as a camp counselor and dance instructor and the beginning of university singing karaoke in bars with the same group of people I may have as well discovered in the lost and found bin.

Some were core friends, the kind of who have coached me through everything from a tampon insertion to an unrequited obsession with a boy who I assumed harbored profoundly negative thoughts about my arm fat. The other friends were girls whose last names I did not know but we still felt each other up in an attempt to experiment with our fluid sexualities but mostly to compare bodies because I've always been worried about the shape of my breasts ("Girl, I read in *Cosmo* there are seven types of breasts, and you're just bell-shaped, you're not saggy I swear!!"). I soothed others in an attempt to soothe myself, as one does.

My friends were often low on cash, so I pretended I was, too. I was embarrassed by my suburban privilege. No one wants to hear about how much your parents love you. My seemingly ideal upbringing made me as exciting as filing taxes on time.

I wanted to know what it felt like to be young and lost and uncertain about my five-year plan. Misery loves company, and I thought that couldn't be truer for The Interesting. I thought I wouldn't be able to keep these friends around if I couldn't find anything troubling to talk about. It's always hard for someone to confide in you about their pain—which they inevitably had—when I was raised by housekeepers and got a yearly birthday shopping spree—which I did, and still do.

We'd go to house parties in Montreal's Notre-Dame-de-Grâce (NDG) along Sherbrooke Street West, a predominantly English-speaking residential borough in a French-speaking city that feels like one big living room with traffic lights. I hesitate to call anything a party unless I've dragged several women to the bathroom with me. I've convinced myself that we are biologically unable to expel urine without the presence of another vagina owner, and that is beautiful on every level. Bathrooms are a dangerous place to venture alone. Often there is no toilet paper left. Often someone creepy follows me in. Often there is no bathroom altogether, and I need someone to stand guard while I squat in an alley.

In the space between the toilet where I sat once I broke the seal and the bathroom door stood Megan, Jill, Ella, Sabrina, Jenna, and Carly (all who have last names) and Sarah, Elizabeth, Catherine, and Melissa (all who don't). Sam, Oliver, Brett, and Tom were the boys I could rely on to pretend I was dating when a creep approached me. It certainly didn't hurt that they were my de facto designated drivers in case we needed to make a swift escape to another living room in NDG.

The ecosystem operated the same way every Saturday night, and Friday night, too, if I wasn't too lethargic from a heavy Shabbat dinner. Boys playing Pink Floyd on acoustic guitar were looking for love and affection, and we were ready to give that to them in the quest for love and affection of our own. Montreal house parties meant kissing boys because they were playing acoustic guitar and kissing girls because said boys with acoustic guitars were watching.

Usually, the weed-induced paranoia kicked in so hard I had to go to the bathroom and touch my face to ensure it was still there, but the way each living room was organized the same way provided comfort: there was a coffee table littered with green weed shake rich in THC crystals illuminating the dim room like fairy lights. There were Société de transport de Montréal bus transfers rolled into filters. They topped off burrito-sized joints so smokey the night looked like you'd just woken up with crust in your eyes. But you could always smoke it Jamaican-style if you didn't care. You could lock yourself in a bathroom with the shower running on hot, hot heat, the St. Ive's apricot-scented mist in the air bridging the gap between who you once were and who you are now.

In NDG, boys blew weed smoke into girls' mouths as a mating ritual. There was a hookah off in the corner for those who opted to methodically practice their ring-shaped exhales and thus who had every intention of dying alone. These boys, without fail, wore chains attached to their wallets, studded black leather bracelets around their wrists, and T-shirts boasting bands that were cool for maybe two weeks in 1997 covering their size AA male breasts. Their hair was full, curly, and black, and it dipped down their temples and chins like an overweight man's hug. It would feel so good to run my hands through their hair, I thought, the way it felt so good to touch my face in front of the mirror when I was high to confirm I was alive.

The tattered beige couches at these parties with blobs of cotton prairie-dogging their way out were something you'd find in the "free stuff" section on Craigslist. They were special because it was very obvious several generations of children had been conceived on each of those couches. I never sat at these parties because it crushed the full expression of my libido during my perennial mating season. My veins, a warm bath of vodka, and blood.

Kids I'd only vaguely seen on the bus ran up to me with open arms when I walked into these parties, demanding I take a sip of their drink, which at the time was nice because it meant I didn't need to nervously shift around a *depanneur* and use a fake ID. My mom checked her liquor cabinets, so that was out of the question.

Drinks were nail polish–remover strong. My friends and I were the first to start dancing, which is actually an underestimated way of saying we used each other as poles to wrap our legs up against like poison ivy leaves on a countryside fence. My nails were painted black and they were chipped, and I loved how it was an artistic manifestation of my self-sabotage. I was the star of my own Ke$ha video well before I knew who she was.

My parents warned me about taking the bus on my own once the sky turned black. They had heard mythical tales of women getting assaulted late at night, of men cornering them into something farfetched and cliché like a bush, commenting on their bodies, following them home. I wouldn't dare deviate from their wish lest I become an even bigger, blacker chipped–nail polish sheep in the family. In truth, I spent the majority of my youth, as young as age seven, getting cat-called. But I use that cutesy name hesitantly since it reduces women to animals and legitimizes verbal assault.

At the time, I only knew of one friend who was viciously attacked while inebriated on something someone slipped in her drink.

Once she rubbed her sleepy eyes open and noticed her nail beds were gone, she knew something was wrong. The circumference of her anus was scratched, and her eye was the shape and size of a plum. But that happened in Milan and Milan seemed so far away. For someone very confused about where I stood on the social hierarchy, I was certain about one thing: even though I felt I deserved to be harmed, I seemed to be impervious to any real signs of it.

Jewish parents love you so much you wouldn't dare disappoint them. So when my parents told me to do something that would protect me or teach me how to grow up, I listened (when it was time to make my bed or take out the recycling, though, I handed them an annotated essay as to why I was unfortunately unavailable at that time).

My friends and I were so protected. Incubator-in-the-neonatal-unit-at-eighteen-years-old-protected. We make jokes about disobedient kids who haven't gotten enough hugs. We were hugged too much. Our parents loved us until we felt asphyxiated by the weight of their gefilte-fleshy arms, and we wouldn't have had it any other way. There wasn't any room in our Jewish suburban bubble for foreign bodies. But still, I took lifts from Sam. He was the only one whose parents never made him pay for gas, so I never felt bad. He taught his parakeet how to say "fuck off" and that was a special brand of pet parenting that resonated with me on a cellular level. He blasted comedy tapes as loud as I wanted and was obsessed with my toilet humor, and when you're the only girl you know who wants to hear about your new butt-wiping trick in vivid detail, it's refreshing for once to not feel so alone. I was a version of myself around him that I actually liked—or at the very least, didn't despise.

But otherwise, I wasn't lost—I was free. In two weeks, I would be an undergraduate student in journalism and creative writing, programs where I immediately checked the name on the envelope to ensure they had sent the acceptance to the right person.

To know what I wanted so fervently was liberating. It provided purpose. So I rewarded myself by trying, for the first time, not to care.

University's little ritual called Frosh Week is where we learned to chug our first beer. It's where we play "just the tip." It's where incoming students spend a week on and off campus playing icebreaker games, cheering for god-knows-what, ripping Frosh T-shirts in ways that conveniently expose cleavage (guilty but not sorry), and drinking booze until we're disoriented enough to agree to another day of recreational self-induced alcohol poisoning. Beer for a snack, beer for lunch, and beer if you just needed something to do with your hands if there was no one to fondle at that very moment.

On the second day, our Frosh leaders herded my group and me onto a yellow school bus bound for a summer camp up north where I used to work as a dancer. Sam sat beside me for the 2.5-hour ride. Geographically speaking, I felt safe. I knew my way down the dusty gravel road to the dining hall, my way to the bunks covered with bubble-lettered names of classmates who called me a nudist in high school because I didn't think it was fair that only guys could change in the hallways before gym class. I was the type to ferociously make out with boys at my locker because I didn't think there was anything wrong with merging your face with another face in an effort to feel a positive feeling.

I was never much of a beer drinker, but as they say, when in hell! (To answer your question, Tucker Max: Yes, it's on the menu). Shirtless boys handed me beers faster than I could drink. "Chug! Don't be a pussy!" they shouted.

To own a pussy is acceptable. To be one is not. Spitters are quitters.

On that first night of Frosh, I can't tell you how many beers I had. I poured them down my throat out of my uvula's sight in quick succession so my gag reflexes wouldn't relegate me to "pussy" territory (and also I liken the taste to what I imagine is challah dipped in piss, so the less time swiveling it around my taste buds, the better).

I grinded up against boys I'd only met one brief Facebook stalk many moons ago, my legs surrounding theirs like poison ivy up a countryside fence. A dance to some Pitbull song with a boy named Colin led to a feral make out in the forest. The whole thing was out-of-body yet pleasant. He was an entrepreneur, more colloquially known as a start-up bro. Though not my usual suspect, I enthusiastically consented to the good, clean, kosher fun we had while branches sodomized me and leaves left me with a rash dotting my calves.

Other boys saw me kissing this person through an opening within the deep green leaves and interpreted it as an invitation to wait in line. One person I had never seen before grabbed me by the waist and led me to a hut that stored kayaks and canoes on the beach. He used its wall to reenact doggy-style sex on me to the beat of "Papa Americano," fully clothed, but as I tried to pry myself from the cage he created with his forearms that surrounded my head, I was stripped naked with shame. He laughed maniacally as I ran through the sand toward the crowd. It was the kind of running that only takes place in a dream—the faster you want to go, the more likely you are to stay in one place.

I couldn't go back to my bunk because it was dark and I was alone without a flashlight, so I stood motionless on the beach swarming with sweaty loud bodies. I held my breath and looked into the navy night sky, my stillness an invisibility tactic. I realized there was no winning.

"Don't just stand there, sexy girl. Come sit on my lap," said a deep, slurred voice. I turned around. He must have been in an online elective, because I only remember ever seeing him during an exam before this, not an in-class lecture. He pushed me to the ground. I was too drunk to tell if it was a flirty or violent push. Either way, it didn't hurt because at my height, there's not much room to fall.

The drunker I got, the number I became to this person's touch. Clinical. Deliberate. When you reduce human interactions to procedures, they become less sexy and more scientific. He touched—or did he fondle?—my chest above my pink American Eagle hoodie in ways reserved for gynecologists. Not that a woman's outfit should ever serve as a way to explain why some are treated one way and others another. I wanted to speak, to yell, to cry, but the words, like my legs through the sand, sank deeper and deeper. Instead, I backed away into the night, floating in a sea of bodies.

* * *

I was lightheaded enough to feel the sand puncturing the underbelly of my toenails as I made my way toward the bunks, this time drunk enough to trust my legs to carry the rest of me where I thought I needed to go. My senses were swept away with the waves. I gave in and became a passenger in my own experience.

I walked into my bunk to find Sam there waiting for me, walking around in circles barefoot. It was dark and his chubby silhouette eclipsed the streetlamps that illuminated the dusty path. I felt the relief of a toddler reuniting with her mother after thirty whole minutes lost in a Walmart.

"Here, I brought you a towel," he said, draping it around me as if he were awarding me with a medal. The cotton felt heavy on my neck, but I couldn't feel each soft fiber like I knew I should have.

"Where were you? You left me all alone out there. You told me you'd stick with me the whole week," I said. "Fucking animals out here. I want to go home."

"I knew you'd be fine! Everyone loves you! I'm sure you had a great time!" he said, patting the top of my head.

"I hooked up with Colin, so I guess it wasn't that bad. I mean, you win some you lose some," I said.

"Ewww, why would you hook up with him? That's disgusting. I'm officially never talking to you again," he said, as he did jokingly every time I confided in him about that kind of stuff.

"Fuck off. First you desert me then you totally brush me off. Let's find you a nice Jewish girl, okay?" I said.

"Okay, but only if she has wild curly hair and never wears makeup," he said.

"Done," I nodded. "I'm showering. I feel disgusting. You in?"

I was conscious enough to recall hopping into the shower stall with my clothes on, undressing, and hanging my bicycle shorts and hoodie up on the hook beside it. Someone had left a bottle of men's Nivea body wash on the tile floor. I lathered it as deep as I could to the bone in an attempt to scrape away the past forty-five minutes of leaves and beer and bodies. I emerged sopping wet with my towel wrapped around me, acutely aware of the impact exposing bare shoulders to a male friend might have. A male friend who once sat me down in a Wendy's parking lot and told me I could change the world.

How I returned to the cabin could be anyone's guess. Through the cataracts of my drunken daze I saw a fleshy, rotund mass engulf my hip bones. My skull ricocheted off the metal headboard with each thrust. Under the weight of his stout body, I was a shipwreck sinking deeper and deeper into the dusty bare mattress. Only in my mind could I pry myself from him. It was the kind of prying that only takes place in a dream—the faster you want to go, the more likely you are to stay in one place. Rather than crying for help, I devoted all my mental faculties to staying alive. I disassociated like a woman might do when she's in labor. I left my body out of shame and disgust, hoping that if I went to sleep, he'd go away or I'd become someone else. The only thing confirming my existence was blood.

I couldn't bear the look of him the next day as we went rafting with the other Froshies in a town nearby. There was a palpable smugness to his shitty sunburnt face as he laid heavily belly-first on a red raft. It was all too evocative of the single image my mind could conceive of the night before. I kept my distance, ensuring the wind never drifted me less than several feet away from him. I anticipated he'd confront me. I thought I had done something wrong. Was it because I was wearing shorts? Was it my shoulders? Was I the girl with curly hair and no makeup?

Like some pathetic kindergartener, I told Brandon, my Frosh leader, that I felt sick and wanted to go home.

"Sure, no worries, Mariss. Let's get you on a bus back. Mind waiting a couple hours?"

"Not a problem at all," I said.

I sat on a curb near the camp office running my heels through the dusty gravel ground as I waited and waited and waited some more. I became aware of each wrinkle, beauty mark, and goose bump on my body. This body—the one that I had spent hours a day nurturing with yoga and kale and sleep—let me down. True to form, this somehow did not surprise me. It was always when I had high hopes for my body that it failed me.

I was, in fact, a pussy, both reduced to the body part and unable, that night, to chug beers without consequences like the rowdy men were able to do. I had chugged all those beers for nothing. The boys whose identities I tried to reduce to

Facebook profiles with grabby hands and wet tongues told me so. If they had the power to make me feel small, they must have been right. And all I got were empty beer calories and trust issues.

I had an entire yellow school bus to myself. I spent an hour and a half peeling off layers of my nail beds, splitting my split ends and pulling out arm hairs one by one.

I was so excited to be home I kissed my kitchen counters and sniffed the walls. I peed with the door open, succeeding at repressing the hellscape into which my vagina had gotten me a day before.

I thought I was home free, literally, until I saw my ex-boyfriend ride his bike past my window. The same one who, on that very street five months prior, had to chug a bunch of beer before a Passover seder in order to bear the idea of sitting around a table with my family. The same one who told me not to become a journalist so as not to become more of a problem than I already was.

"I heard you had fun," he cried out from across the street as I opened my front door to go for a walk.

"What?" I asked, genuinely confused about what he was talking about.

"You're pretty dumb to think I wouldn't find out," he said.

"Okay . . . why are you here?"

"Before I tell you, you should really know he's telling everyone. Bragging that you wanted it and loved it. Why am I not surprised, you fucking whore?"

"You need to stop."

21

"Sorry, I can't help it," he said with a tone that reeked of evil. "I just find it so hilarious. You and him. Classic!"

"Okay, that's nice. I'm gonna go now. Bye."

"No, wait up," he said. "I'm just joking. You know I would never say anything to intentionally hurt you."

"Well, you literally just showed up to my house to harass me. Your idea of a joke is pretty dumb."

"Wow, quit being such a bitch," he said.

Now I was starting to get scared.

"Alright, what would it take for you to leave?" I asked.

"Funny you ask," he said. "Give me your Frosh bracelet." It was the red piece of plastic we wore around our wrists that allowed us entry into events serving free alcohol.

"Sorry, I threw it out," I replied.

"Doesn't matter. Get it for me. Do what it takes or I'm not leaving."

"It's in the garbage. Don't be an animal."

"You're not using it anymore. What do you care?"

"I just don't think you need it, that's all."

"Uh, wrong. Free booze cruise, free bitches. Plus, I want to see Sam and give him a high five. I fucking hate him but we're Eskimo Brothers now and that's cool."

"Okay, that's enough out of you. Bye, for real this time."

Good-byes are never "for real this time." He walked up my front steps, pushed past me, and opened the lid to my tall blue recycling bin, peaking his head into the filthy void.

"Are you fucking kidding me?" I asked, completely bewildered as I watched on.

"Not one bit. Let me in. I'm searching your garbage bins."

And just like that, he reduced himself to an alley raccoon as he ran sprints across my hallway from garbage to garbage. He sunk his hairy, tanned arms into each bin rummaging for that ripped red bracelet. Finally, he got to my bedroom and dumped out a bin full of used Kleenex, gum wrappers, and dirty menstrual pads across the floor.

"I knew I'd find it," he said proudly, holding it up like a garter belt he had ripped off his bride's thigh.

He used a piece of tape on my dresser to fasten the ripped bracelet onto his wrist.

"I promise to put this to good use," he said with a wink.

I remained silent because anything I said could and would be used against me in a proverbial court of law. I watched him cycle off into the distance wearing the one piece of evidence left that I had attended Frosh. Without that red bracelet, my assault was a memory, and no one believes memories. Trauma warps memories and memories themselves fade. My memory was a red ripped bracelet at the bottom of the trash.

I wondered if that was what it felt like to be robbed at gunpoint. It's not that I would have any use for the bracelet. He could have it. But like a thief in the dark of night, I didn't know what other types of crimes he'd commit with his newfound weapon. He had no qualms breaking into my house, the one place left I felt safe. In letting him steal from me, I felt responsible for whatever he would inevitably do to other women, just like Sam did to me.

I didn't speak to Sam until a week later when I needed a designated driver to another one of those infamous parties. I was still in denial that it even happened, and I thought that confronting him or cutting off contact would cement the truth in reality. I don't remember our first interactions, only the feelings I had surrounding them. I experienced a pulsating discomfort in my sternum as I climbed into the backseat of his car, careful to avoid as many surfaces as possible. When I am repulsed by a guy, I often joke that my vagina feels like it has stapled itself shut. Here, my vagina fell the fuck off. I asked Sam to turn up the comedy tapes blasting from his shitty speakers to drown out the loud voices in my brain.

For four years, I continued to take lifts from him. On the way to another party, we both stopped to pee in an alley. It had occurred to me at that moment that my genitals—or rather my person—should never be within close proximity to him ever again.

"That thing that happened," I stammered, "that should have never happened and every time I think about it, I want to die."

By the time I had admitted to myself that it was far from consensual, I couldn't get a rape kit because there was no more forensic evidence on me to test. I couldn't go to a doctor and get a sexually transmitted infection test because in a fit of debilitating anxiety I was not able to leave my bed. I couldn't report the incident to law enforcement because the part I mentally blocked out—the part that faded with memory the harder it crushed my ribs—would be required information at a court proceeding, further robbing me of any sort of authority I had over my own experience. I couldn't report it to the school's administration because my grades and social standing were more important than my safety. Plus, who would believe me?

What I could do, however, was lie down, my legs fastened in stirrups, and look up at the fluorescent ceiling lights until Dr. Frontenac shuffled me out the door and gave me what I thought was some semblance of my body back when he inserted the IUD. Right then, I made an executive decision about my vagina and regardless of what it was, it was empowering as hell. My vagina was still attached to me, sitting still with me at exams that sometimes I aced and sometimes I didn't. It bled on schedule, sometimes in rhythmic waves and other times in staccato pulses, reminding me I was alive. But it was mine, and if we can't rely on anything from friends to birth control, we have ourselves. And that is often enough.

It wasn't until news broke that former Hollywood producer Harvey Weinstein was convicted of raping and assaulting actresses who worked under him that I even considered my experience rape. I had blamed myself all along. Survivors began outing their attackers in droves, one after the other, until it felt like we had swept the world clean of men who thought they could get away with the unspeakable.

But then there was me. Silent. Wanting so desperately to speak, to yell, to cry, but the words wouldn't come out.

Last I heard about Sam he was incarcerated in Cambodia for punching a tuk tuk driver in the face. In hoarding my secret, I felt complicit. Like a bad feminist, truly harkening to Roxane Gay's book I'd read that month. What was supposed to be cathartic further stimulated my rage. I wrote a deeply investigative piece for *Teen Vogue* about the ways in which physicians and government officials financially exploit rape victims, further exacerbating their trauma. For *Allure*, I covered the trend of alleged male abusers and rapists receiving punishments far softer than their crimes. My body and I have endured quite some heavy stuff. But if I hadn't, I wouldn't appreciate wins—big and small—like I do now. Sure, I'm unable to ride the elevator with a member of the opposite sex without wanting to both cover up *and* throw up, but I can now ace meetings at iconic magazine publishing houses, cross finish lines by way of chafed thighs, and call myself out on the self-destructive lies I was once conditioned to tell myself. And if that still means having to take the stairs once in a while, so be it. We can all use a little extra cardio. Though, sometimes that cardio comes in the form of a half-marathon four hours after bleeding out on my kitchen floor.

Chapter 2

MISSION IMPOSTOR SYNDROME

I 'll never be ready to write a book. I have yet to wake up and say "I have garnered enough wisdom over the last quarter of a century to put my thoughts down on a document so long it might crash the MacBook I dipped into my Bat Mitzvah fund to buy, send it to a publisher, and print it into a million little copies, only for it to be forever littered across the Pinterest-worthy bookshelves of hipster millennials across the world who are definitely way cooler than me."

When we tweet about something awful that's happened to us, it's punctuated by "a memoir." Fell into a puddle and now everyone thinks I peed, a memoir. Went to the gym, forgot my sneakers, and accidentally liked a photo on my ex's Instagram from seventy-six weeks ago, a memoir. Thought it was herpes, but nope! Just some farmer's market jam, a memoir.

Talking about myself unironically is as comfortable as receiving a Taser-administered Pap smear. No one wants to hear the young person preach from a soapbox, even when it's of the "Honey I Washed the Kids" vegan and cruelty-free Lush variety. No one cares about the inner monologue of an adolennial. I used to think of my life as a series of soaked menstrual pads and failed math tests. But in searching for relatable things to write about for my various columns, I've learned that's not quite the case.

I grew up in Côte-Saint-Luc, Quebec, one of the most densely populated Jewish neighborhoods in the world. And when I say Jewish, I mean *Jewish*. So Jewish, in fact, that my jogging itinerary relied on passing the fewest synagogues possible. After all, buoyant breasts aren't exactly kosher for Passover, or ever. (Not that the Hasidic men would have seen them anyways. They aren't allowed to make eye contact with members of the opposite sex. Acknowledging their presence is still under debate).

I use my jogging abilities as a yardstick to identify points in time. For instance, in grade eight, my dad would stretch his hamstrings as I laced up my sneakers, then ushered me up Mackle Road until Heywood Avenue and back.

I couldn't make it until McAlear before yelling at him to call an ambulance in strong language that impressed even a gentle and conservative guy like him. He would run far ahead of me but immediately turn back after about half a block so as not to make me feel bad for being out of shape.

He grew up playing baseball and I'm confident my mother would issue him a hall pass to fulfill his lifelong dream of spring training with former Montreal Expos' right fielder Vladimir Guerrero. So as not to exacerbate the punctured wound in his soul attributed to living in a city without a baseball team anymore, I've never mentioned that the Jamaican-born athlete's kiss on my right cheek at age five was the definitive start of my sexual awakening.

The more hamstrings and Achilles tendons he tore playing softball with fellow nerdy chartered accountants, the less jogging became the glue that held us together. That's when I was left to my own devices, and things got real messy.

At eighteen, I blasted bands like As I Lay Dying, Dying Fetus, and Anal Cunt from my iPod loud enough to drown out the sound of my heavy breathing. I didn't need any more reminders I was suffering. Blisters down to the bone were a form of self-mutilation I could perform on the daily without having to group myself into the category of "cutters." Because that would mean I objectively, immediately, needed to seek help, and of course, I was too busy jogging to make the time to call the kid's helpline on a milk carton.

I was ten years old when I had a day off from private Hebrew school. It was two in the afternoon in December, and I remember this because you remember Montreal winters even if they kill you. I had lunch at noon and I read in a magazine with Mandy Moore on the cover that you should eat every three hours for an efficient metabolism. I wasn't due for another hour, but my hunger bordered on Yom Kippur levels. At that age, I couldn't tell you a single thing about the socioeconomic politics inherent in Polly Pockets, but I could calculate the caloric value of any and all foods and condiments. Still couldn't parlay that into a job as a doctor. My parents have forgiven me, but I have my doubts.

My stomach rumbled as I glided my hands across each quadrant of my torso. Two ribs and two hipbones meant four opportunities to congratulate myself as they protruded even more than they did the week before. My Bat Mitzvah was seven months away and my size-two pink floral Betsey Johnson dress was unforgiving against my budding breasts and fleshy thighs. Having to suck in while reading my *d'var torah* on the *bima* meant I would have had to choke out former Israeli prime minister Golda Meir's impact on the state of Israel mid-gasp for oxygen. She deserved more respect than that.

The purple fleece Gap Kids sweatpants I was currently wearing, however, were a size large. But you couldn't have even bribed me with limited-edition Barbies to keep the label on. I didn't even want the skeletons in my closet to know I was anything but a small at all times. I hated being human and the hunger that accompanied it. Hunger was a need. Need was a weakness. But there were Krispy Kreme donuts on the kitchen counter, taunting me in all their two hundred-calorie glory. My mother put them there without the faintest clue they'd spark a week-long spiral.

Never been one to succumb to peer pressure—or spouse or child pressure—she miraculously remained pragmatic in a home whose walls reverberated with the constant buzz of disordered eating talk. As a daughter of two Holocaust survivors, her perception of food is very much a matter of "Waste not, want not" and "You can all go fuck yourselves because my body after two children is bangin' and I don't need a PhD in biochemistry to figure that out, even though I do conveniently have one."

She told me anything in moderation was fine. But my mother loved me so much she saw past my stomach rolls and back fat. I didn't trust her to have my best body dysmorphia interest in mind.

Still, I ate a donut so fast I barely chewed.

Weakness. Bad. Failure. Human. These words flashed through my mind like billboards dotting the highway, making a spectacle of me eating like some circus freak in a cage at a county fair. One person's sexual fetish is another Jewish girl's nightmare.

It took me twenty years to figure out why the donut freaked me out, but we'll get to that later. In that moment, all that mattered was undoing the damage I had done. So I resorted to the only quick fix I knew: I peeled open that issue of *Seventeen* magazine, my hands trembling against the words on the page that ultimately couldn't help me— Mandy Moore's beauty secrets, how to ace your next test, take this quiz to find out if your friendship will survive high

31

school. Forget it. I've been told my skin is so soft I definitely receive daily facials of the ejaculatory ilk. My grades were high enough to enjoy Pink Floyd on vinyl. Diana and I admitted to each other in the schoolyard the week before that it felt good to pull rogue hairs out of our buttholes after the shower, so I didn't need a quiz to tell me we were inseparable at that point.

My trembling fingers finally landed on a two-page spread featuring cartoonish girls in purple and pink shorts performing basic yoga poses. "Designed to detox the body and mind . . . " "Burn calories and gain energy . . . " "Get the body you've always wanted . . . "

You could have sold me cow dung with those buzz phrases alone.

The girls had knees so bony they resembled wrist watches. Their clavicles were so deep they could sneak notes into an exam. I didn't see a modicum of myself in these pencil-shaded drawings—unless you count the part where we both appropriate a time-honored cultural practice as an attempt to become better versions of ourselves.

Their downward dogs were pointy pyramids. Their savasanas were straight thin lines. So straight, in fact, you could determine their measurements by using the formula $y=ax+b$, where $a=0$. I was a kid's large, at best a two. Not yet a zero, not yet a woman.

The donut in me didn't budge as I mentally tracked its whereabouts in my digestive tract. I felt it sit inside me like a tumor, spreading its cancerous fat down to my breasts and thighs and love handles, a body part whose name I never understood because there is nothing loveable about handling them whatsoever. If food babies were real, I wanted an abortion.

I ripped Mandy Moore's porcelain face in half for no apparent reason other than it seemed like something Avril Lavigne would do when she's angry in a music video. *She's thin and makes good music ergo probably knows what she's doing*, I thought. My angst-ridden display of athleticism was cathartic for a whole second until I remembered I was still me, trapped in my same size large no matter how tightly I closed my eyes, willing the weight away.

I was still me in my training bra. I was still me with a Jew-'fro mound of pubic hair and armpits to match. I was still me but with hips so childbearing I could birth a child my size. I was still me but so far from whom I wanted to be.

So I ran toward her, searching for a solution in my slush-filled winter boots and ripped cobalt blue snowsuit. It was the first time I had ever left the house without telling my parents in fully annotated detail where I would be and with whom. I would never be ready, so I said the *sh'ma Israel* under my hastening breath, and just ran.

I leapt over heaps of yellow snow and bolted down the quiet block toward nothing. I probably got the idea to run my breasts away from a shitty movie. Instead they just throbbed under the flimsy padding of my Gap Kids training bra. I took long strides like I was Olympian gymnast Gabby Douglas performing air splits because in those moments my inner thighs were miles apart. I counted each step to make the seconds go by faster. It felt like I was running in a dream, where your legs buckle in invisible quicksand but you have a whole marathon left inside of you. If I couldn't be like the quite literal stick figures in my favorite magazine, I might as well run trying.

My legs gave out, and I collapsed. Alone, I heaved in the fetal position on the icy sidewalk somewhere on the corner of Palmer and Mathers. Even though I had run in a straight line, I had no idea where I was or what I was doing. Either I was a few months away from getting my period for the first time (I was), or I was completely delusional for thinking pain could erase my past or that my past was bad to begin with (both of these things are true).

I wasn't scared of the donut. I was scared of growing up and becoming a woman and all that it seemed to entail, like lugging around a growing body and a growing number of responsibilities. If my breasts complicated so much as a yoga pose, I couldn't imagine what sort of physical and psychological implications they'd have in my everyday life.

Sure, magazines warned me about these "bodily transformations" I speak of, but nothing could have prepared me for the complete meltdown that ensued when I finally gave in to who I was becoming. Being a woman is hard, but becoming one is even harder.

As an older sister, I was always my own experiment rat. I didn't have anyone familiar in my demographic to turn to about whether leggings classify as pants or whether or not it's possible to get pregnant from giving a hand job.

Come age twenty-five, I had to dig through the white male noise just to find one account of a young woman like me, as odd as me. I look back on my ten-year-old self who reduced her self-worth to her inability to resemble a cartoon character peppered with headlines that lured her in to be something else. I pride myself on knowing how to write clickable copy without triggering a full-blown eating disorder. I write because I never want another kid alone and confused in their bedroom to have to feel that way again.

We will continue to feel like shit about ourselves until it's A-OK for young people to share their experiences. My two female Canadian literary crushes, Monica Heisey and Scaachi Khoul, received similar reviews about their debut memoirs. The overarching feedback was that the millennial memoir is by design "self-indulgent." And why is that a bad thing? When millennials aren't privy to the lives of other millennials, we begin to think we're doing far worse in life than we actually are. And anyone who doesn't eat cold pizza standing up at four in the morning is not someone with which you have much in common anyway.

We're told to celebrate ourselves, but the moment we're vocal, and even in a self-deprecating way like my literary crushes, no less—we're told to cross our proverbial legs. The messages about how to feel about ourselves both in language and in pop culture are so nuanced that it feels like we cannot win. Self-conscious: bad. Self-esteem: good. Self-centered: bad. Selfless: good. Selfish: bad.

Beyoncé, bless her soul, is allowed to bask in a photoshoot with her bursting belly as the centerpiece. But moments after us Earthlings so much as upload a few quick timeline posts, Jenny from eighth grade biology has already screenshotted it to four nightmare girls from high school saying that our newborns' smiles "really puts the chew in Chewbacca." The female social hierarchy is not going to go away, and it shouldn't, because striving to become Beyoncé is as fulfilling a full-time job as any. It might be lonely at the top, but Christ is it confusing trying to get there.

In the spirit of the world going to shit, there's only one option: to love ourselves for putting up with an oppressive system that inherently wants to make us feel miserable about ourselves so they can sell us Lululemon leggings and detox tea. We did not sign up for this! We were launched via an umbilical cord lasso straight out of the cervix into a cold, hard world that is continuously testing our strength with tampon taxes, institutionalized racism, soaring avocado prices, and (at the time of this writing) a human ballsack for an American president! And when things are hard enough as it is, directing criticism inward is more exhausting than trying to get through a Pilates YouTube video on Yom Kippur (still repenting for that one on a spiritual level), or a couple yoga poses when you're ten and want to throw your changing body in the garbage with empty donut wrappers you want gone forever.

Don't love yourself because it's better than the alternative. Celebrate who you are because no one will ever be able to experience what it's like to be you. Who's had to deal with sitting in a pile of period sludge with the manual dexterity of a car mechanic? Who made the promise to never respond to a 2:00 a.m. "u up?" text again AND ACTUALLY FOLLOWED THROUGH? Who made it this far reasonably intact? You. That's who. And that's worthy of a celebration complete with a guest list and tuna tartare.

It's taken me a quarter of a century to grow comfortable with the fact that life doesn't have to be miserable—and it's still a work in progress. Up until now, my brain worked on self-hating autopilot. When I told my doctor I felt that way, he had me complete the Goldberg depression test. On a scale from "not at all" to "to a great extent," I reported on sleeping habits, interest in activities that used to mean a lot to me, and whether I had devised a plan to end my own life.

"Marissa, I'm . . . I'm . . . speechless," my doctor said.

He looked at my score like he'd just found something vile on a colonoscopy scan. He wrote me a prescription for the highest dose of the antidepressant Cipralex, and later in my treatment to counteract the daily noon nap and inability to orgasm, Wellbutrin. I went home and cut the tiny white pill in half with a bread knife. Two weeks later, the sun became brighter and sweets became sweeter. I tell fellow SSRI-ers on Reddit forums that I am alive today because of those jagged little pills. But the guilt sets in once I catch myself existing within a happy moment. It's not like I actually complete the cognitive behavioral therapy homework my therapist issues at the end of each session. These pills end up doing the work *for* me, robbing me of any ability to take credit for my own happiness or anything of value that materializes from said happiness. It's like that creeping sense of impostor syndrome that impedes my ability to take full credit for things people call my "accomplishments." Then again, what do I know?

Quite a bit to some people, apparently.

I've been asked to speak as a relationship expert in the capacity of everything from a radio panelist to a journalist to an open-eared best friend. Never do I feel qualified. Never do I feel like I have anything new to say. What kind of idiot asks me to weigh in on relationships on a public platform when that morning I logged onto a guy's email and went through two years of junk mail on the off chance some Other Woman sent him nudes? If the saying is "You are who you date!" (that's probably not a saying at all, but I'm screwed if it is), then I'd be a self-loathing misogynist who'd rather eat Tom Brady's sweaty butthole than a woman's freshly baked labia (which is fine!!!!!). I'd be reduced to the—I say this lightly—*men* I've dated. Let's take a bad trip down men lane:

1. There was that time I was in love with a guy who didn't dump me like a pile of on-fire diapers in the trash once, but six times. And I thought I deserved it, because who would ever in their right mind date a girl who listens to death metal? Idiot McGee gave me his password, so I found out he also sent pictures of his penis to women on Craigslist, which is Tinder for Serial Killers™. I give the photography on those a solid four out of ten. The lighting was fine, but the angles needed work.

2. There was the Scientologist. Enough said.

3. There was that person who was so nervous about spending Passover at my parents' house that he

chugged several beers on the sidewalk. He fingered his sister in the bath as a kid. He said I'd be "way hotter, like a ten" if I chose journalism instead of English literature as my major. He preferred peeing in sinks over toilets. Chalking this up to "eco-friendly" instead of "flag redder than communism" is on me.

4. There was that person who used his money selling weed to buy me Jay-Z tickets for my birthday, which, when you think about it, needs to be made into a John Green novel. But my point remains.

These men were flawed, but I excused them for it. Nay, celebrated them. They did things that upset me constantly, and I stuck by them, further reaffirming just how in charge they were. Sure, they needed fixing. But "I could be [their] hero, baby." It was romantic and exciting to get involved with people who were so fucked up and wrong for me I thought of them as Pinterest art projects for a rainy day. We could be boring on our porch rocking chairs when we're sixty. Now, let's get into a fight in the middle of a mutual friends' dinner party just to feel alive.

Like you, I've spent years justifying why other people are right and I am wrong, or why they are more right than me. I have continuously placed other people's values above mine in a way that hacked away at my self-esteem with an ice pick until the thought of being in public or having a conversation with another human made me feel like an open, raw wound. But it takes a lot of self-awareness to admit I don't have any, so I've got that going for me!

It's not so much the self-esteem issues that made me feel like the jam between your toes after a long jog. C'mon, that's so '90s! It's the impostor syndrome I ranted about in the introduction, a universal phenomenon you likely suffer from if women's magazines and rom-coms starring Jennifer Aniston sent you cryptic messages all your life that you weren't good enough, and you now struggle to come to terms with any sort of personal victories or success. The more successful I get, the harder it is for me to internalize what I've earned or recognize I deserve it. The more workshops I'm invited to teach or the more *New York Times* features I'm asked to write, the more I wonder if this is all just a cruel prank, my true identity as a nose-picking freak who eats the majority of her meals with her hands lingering not far behind.

Tina Fey said it better than I ever could because what to do I know (nothing!!): "The beauty of the impostor syndrome is you vacillate between extreme egomania and a complete feeling of: 'I'm a fraud! Oh God, they're on to me! I'm a fraud!' So you just try to ride the egomania when it comes and enjoy it, and then slide through the idea of fraud." Tina Fey once kissed Amy Schumer at the 2015 Peabody Awards, and Amy Schumer once told me on Twitter she loves my work. If my not-yet-peer-reviewed theory of "we are who we date" (or kiss on stage or tweet at) holds any weight, then what often happens is that the people whose judgments you admire often admire you back. That renders you objectively great. If that's not an invitation to put on your nice underwear, I don't know what is. (Medical disclaimer: external validation isn't sustainable but it's a fun and toxic way to help you understand what it feels like to be valued!).

Research is still mixed on whether there is a true connection between issues of self-esteem and impostor syndrome. Does it matter? Yes. I've never met a single person who, after a couple beers or bong hits, hasn't confided in me about their self-perceived inadequacies. To be sentient is to be self-conscious. Literally. And that shouldn't be the case. Had I known earlier in life I wasn't alone, I may have been able to fast-track my healing. Like, hello, it's easier to find a therapist in Montreal than it is to find dinner reservations on a terrace.

Dr. Valerie Young is a world-renowned expert on impostor syndrome and has extensively studied women's self-limiting patterns. She told me that while self-esteem is characterized as the global sense we have about ourselves, impostor feelings relate specifically to our achievements. And in a world where women continue to struggle to garner the same credit as men for the same type of work, it's no surprise we feel undeserving of our success.

In an effort to understand what the actual fuck was going on inside my brain, I read case studies about the types of women that typically succumb to the impostor plague. It's usually high-achieving women at high levels in their careers. Think of PhD's like Dr. Young herself, lawyers, doctors, and renowned academics. But, much to my Jewish parents' dismay, I am none of those things. I've reached a type of success that many experience but rarely talk about.

41

The kind that no one says is possible. The kind that lands on your lap straight out of college, even before you've had the chance to practice your networking skills at happy hour while you wobble around in a sale-rack pencil skirt from Ann Taylor Loft. But are any of us ever ready for success, happiness, joy, fulfillment, or even contentment? Do any of us ever feel like the talented experts others say we are? Are we mostly just afraid of growing into the people we're meant to be? Is this rhetorical question format starting to make me sound like Carrie Bradshaw who hasn't been relevant since 1997?

Impostor syndrome, an epidemic that so deeply robs budding and seasoned professionals of recognizing their worth, isn't relegated to the workforce. If you're anything like me, it permeates into everything you do: you apologize constantly and it's not because you're Canadian; you hesitate to shell out criticism and advice (because what authority could you possibly have?!); and you don't accept invitations because you assume they're a pity gesture (on more than one occasion I've missed interesting events because I thought someone added me to the Facebook group as an accident). If you're anything like me, you not only believe that you're unworthy of good things happening to you but that you deserve *bad things* to happen to you. Here's why we're both wrong: we are so very worthy of success and happiness just by virtue of us thinking we're not worthy. Those who walk the earth feeling entitled to success by simply existing haven't put in the work like us impostors. Those feelings of fraudulence are humbling. To combat

42

your feelings of fraudulence, I imagine, like me, you try so, so hard to do better and *be* better. To be a little bit more kind and to be a little bit more authentic (even if that means embracing your inner weirdo). You deserve every compliment, every award, and every avocado because you had to contribute something positive to the world before coming to that place of acceptance or victory.

I've been called a weirdo ever since my peers first learned how to talk, but the name really stuck in high school when I would broadcast the state of my bowels and spend entire lunch breaks wordlessly staring at my crush like a serial killer while he played basketball. If it weren't for my insistence on changing out of my gym shorts in the hallway or giving a public speech about why we should all become nudists, I would have blended in. But I didn't. Everything I did, no matter how mundane, elicited some shocked or offended reaction within my friends, family, and teachers. My family talks about their bowels at home—weirdness was how we bonded. It then made no sense to me that my grade-four crush gagged into his hands when I told him greasy Shabbat dinner makes me constipated. It felt counterintuitive to talk in formalities about his hobbies or plans for the weekend. Why couldn't we bypass the bullshit and go straight to the good stuff? The stuff that bonded my family and me?

I pushed those feelings of otherness away and accepted them as a permanent facet of my identity. No one was talking about therapy while I was in high school, so help was out of the question. And plus, being weird felt like a permanent facet of my personality. It seemed like a leap to equate my personality with a mental illness.

I had worn the oddball identity since as early as I can remember: on a hot July afternoon in 1998, I was at Champion's Day Camp proudly showing off my hot pink one-piece bathing suit with thick, holographic silver streaks running through it. I was next in line to slide down the makeshift waterslide that was actually just a Slip 'n Slide draped down a hill. I placed two digits on my jugular vein reveling in how alive the touch of my rapid heartbeat made me feel. I went flying down the slide, my blonde curls swaying in the wind.

But something felt . . . off. Eerily similar to wearing a thong. Only a lot worse.

"AHHHHHH!" I shrieked.

I turned around and looked down. My camp counselor ran up to me and swore in French so I wouldn't understand. But I knew what *merde* meant.

It looked like I had sat in a pool of period blood. My white naked ass looked like the Japanese flag. I had gotten such an intense wedgie on the slide that my bathing suit ripped against the tough crevice of my underaged asshole. My butt cheeks shredded like mozzarella cheese as I slid onto the grass at the bottom of the slide. It's one thing to change in the hallway next to my fellow peers before third period gym class. It's another to be naked and bloody like the day I was born.

I was somehow able to show my face at camp the next day. After all, unfortunate things happen to me more often than not, so this anal event felt very in line with my usual routine. Even before personal brands were a thing, I made it my mission to be okay with being myself—if anything, to make others like me feel not so alone.

* * *

The first time I walked into the high-rise where my therapist's office sat at the top floor, I buried my face in a massive white wool scarf my bubby knitted for me. Even though the coast was clear, I felt like I was walking into an abortion clinic surrounded by violent protesters. I wanted to take this secret to my grave. I was ashamed that I had to pay a professional to help me work through my fears, like they were so severe my network of close friends I've amassed throughout my twenty-three years couldn't do the trick.

The building was located in Westmount, a ritzy Montreal suburb. Each block featured shops that got incrementally farther out of my financial reach: the drug store where I pick up my meds and Essie nail polish, a salad shop called Mandy's where I had to take home the rest of my twenty dollar Waldorf salad because my loud and aggressive crying squashed my appetite, and a lingerie store offering $490 corsets.

On my walk to the office, I passed well-dressed and fully bathed college kids on their commute home. I felt heavy as their eyes lingered on me. They knew. With my studded fanny pack and leggings ripped at the crotch, there was no other reason I'd be crossing their path in that part of town.

I looked down as I bolted through the doors of the

building. If I couldn't be like the stick figures in my favorite magazine or in shape like my dad, I might as well run trying.

The elevator inched toward the top of the building, its floor ricocheting beneath my legs. I hid my numb, cold hands in my sweaty cleavage because we all have our nervous ticks that make us adorably endearing but also unable to face another day asphyxiated with anxiety. I crossed what seemed like a receptionist in that silent and empty hallway, pretending I was lost and on the wrong floor. Only the "crazies" went up to the fifth.

"Hi, I'm Francesca," my therapist greeted me, her glasses hanging off the tip of her nose.

She hadn't said more than three words, and I hated her already.

The room was cold and severe. Her office had the blandness of an accountant's and the walls were the color of chewed barley in a toddler's vomit. I was distracted by the disco-ball diamond occupying the entire lower half of her left ring finger.

"So, Marissa. Tell me what brings you here," she said with a cocky smirk. I felt like I had gotten into trouble with a fellow classmate and was now in an awkward face-off with their parents. She started her script in a way that all cliché shrinks do. With glazed eyes, she swayed her head up and down like a bobblehead action figure as she tuned me out. Where did she go? Probably just counting down the moments until she could score some skinny vanilla lattes and shoot them intravenously just to get through a job she clearly despised.

"Well, let's see," I told her, ripping off a hangnail. "I'm constantly filled with a sense of dread and I feel like I want to die. I can't sleep at night, and when I do, it's a shallow sleep like one eye is open. Well, I start to panic once I get into bed because I feel like I have too much work but also not enough work, know what I mean? And then I need to smoke a joint to calm down, but not like a *joint* joint, more like a one-hit-wonder type thing, hahahaha, and then I tweet something dumb and it gets a thousand retweets but I'm high so I feel like I don't deserve any of the recognition because my sober brain probably isn't that funny, and then I forget that weed makes me panic even more because I'm not sure if my roommate can smell it and is mad at me that it stinks or that I didn't ask her to join, and then I start to freak out when I get hungry because I always forget smoking weed gives me the munchies and I *hate* eating," I rambled, both because I was petrified of what she would think and because I was trying to get my money's worth out of a session that insurance wouldn't cover.

"Am I an addict or just depressed? What are your thoughts on like, Valium, or those things that kill your sex drive but half my friends are on them? Oh yeah, SSRIs. What do you know about SSRIs? Do they increase or diminish appetite? I need to know this," I said. "Your answer determines the entire course of my therapy."

"Slow down, slow down, slow down. Catch your breath. Have you tried melatonin?"

Bitch, what? I didn't speed-walk for half an hour to be introduced to your sorcery. Pharmaceuticals or bust, I thought.

After fifty more minutes of her collecting data out of the Petri dish cesspool that was my psyche, I headed straight to the vitamin and supplement aisle at Walmart. The store was vast and comparatively I was small. Moms compared cereal box nutritional information; students scoped out backpacks. I was out there trying to find the secret to being alive.

I tilted my head a full ninety degrees to see the wall of colorful pills promising to make me better. I got whiplash and calf cramps trying to read all the labels.

For the bulk of our first meeting, I asked Francesca how to stop using substances to make me feel okay. She told me my options ranged from mindfulness strategies to cognitive behavioral therapy to breathing techniques. From the get-go, I knew none of those would work. My anxiety was as real and permanent as my left arm. No amount of challenging my thinking or shutting my eyes to tropical music would fix that. Still, I was tired—so tired—of waking up every morning with an emotional hangover.

"Hi Francesca, sorry, can't remember the dosage you suggested? Let me know, thanks," I sent over text. I wouldn't be a true Canadian if I didn't unnecessarily apologize and give thanks in the same breath.

As I waited for her to respond, which was never quick enough, I paced up and down the aisles identifying products that could conceivably make me better.

Prenatal pills were rich in beautifying biotin and folic acid. My former coworker at the YM-YWHA on Westbury used them to grow her hair out (she was also the type to refresh her wedding registry constantly, but alas). She had shiny chestnut locks and a vested interest in all things heteronormatively female, and what did I know? My hair texture could only reasonably be defined as Jewish—curly enough for the TSA to search it for contraband, and luscious enough to look decent in an Instagram photo once I put on a filthy hour-long podcast and straightened it with a flat iron. But I wasn't standing in the aisles of Walmart to get pretty. I was there to feel normal.

"Start with the lowest dose of melatonin, 5mg," read the text from my therapist. "Keep a journal of your sleep schedule for the week."

Interacting with her outside of her office walls gave her a Siri-like quality. I wanted to shut her off with the push of a button but was probably better off with her guidance lurking in the background. I didn't hate her so much as I hated what she represented—my inability to cope on my own.

"Okay, thanks!" I texted back with fingers covered in hair oil I surreptitiously tested but didn't buy.

I picked up the highest dose, got the hell out of there, and ran toward the person I had always wanted to be.

Within the cloudy depths of your impostor feelings lie pockets of hope more vibrant than any saturated Instagram filter. Whether you go to therapy or bring this book to the beach, you're one page—and maybe one tearful monologue—closer to uniting your acclaimed personal Twitter brand to how you really feel inside.

Your therapist is not you, and maybe even from another generation. They don't know what it's like to put your ~Best Self~ forward on the internet, only to feel like a total disappointment in person (at best, they've sexted in Morse code, rendering at least some of their strategies transferable). You need a peer to mirror the impostor struggle. I'm here to help you escape from the idea that we always need to feel the kind of "perfect" others insist we are. We will not let our impostor syndrome hold us back. We will talk about our impostor syndrome as a way to kick it straight up the rectum, not to replicate the cartoonishly lithe figures in *Seventeen* but to be able to run down the block toward the person you're meant to be without buckling at your knees and tumbling into the fetal position in a yellow mound of snow. Believing that your success is an accident is a lonely feeling. But that loneliness is shared, thereby—surprise!— eliminating it entirely. That loneliness encourages you to find your people, to make your mark. It's your driving force to a life well lived and a life well deserved. If your long-lost classmates from elementary school who used to call you a "fugly slut" (classic!) now continuously ask for professional advice, pull up a chair. If you are somehow not the total failure you anticipated you'd be, prompting an existential identity crisis, I saved you a seat. Over here. In the back. No, dummy. Six o'clock. I'm wearing red pants.

You may have gotten cheated on; you may have picked your nose and your office crush saw; you may have publicly admitted you don't like dogs and now wake up each morning to an inbox full of death threats; you may have the cardiovascular stamina of a shoelace when you find yourself running into the void of a Canadian winter like some low-budget Nickelback video. Shortcomings are the very things that make us grow like voluminous biotin-powered locks, which you probably panic-bought in aisle five at Walmart.

Those feelings of inadequacy, I remind myself, are always tied to my inability to reconcile who I think I am with what I do for a living. If I had a nickel (guess I have Nickelback on the brain) for every hour I spent overanalyzing how others see me instead of trying to be the best I could be, I'd be able to buy a whole Starbucks secret menu unicorn jizz-flavored something or other. Here's what they don't teach you in sex ed: you can pick your nose and be both wildly loved and successful. You can be both weird and worthy. You can have your cake and eat it standing up with your bare hands, too. Settle for self-love because you've exhausted all alternate options, and many, if not all of them, include smoking a joint all alone in your bed that was so strong you accidentally spread weed-infused lube on a granola bar you found in your sock drawer and got way too high on that combination by accident (true story).

Embracing my inner—and outer—weirdo is a feat bumpier than any ass-grating Slip 'n Slide. I still haven't figured out how to accept myself, and maybe I never will. And that's okay. At least it makes for some good, clean, uncomfortable fodder with my crushes. I'd rather you find out I'm a freak right away than divorce me two kids and a mortgage into our relationship. I'd rather be weird because it gives us something to talk about.

Chapter 3

COMING OUT PARTY

I was thirteen when the editor of the school newspaper announced in the daily bulletin that he was looking to feature more creative writing pieces in the next issue. I thought about putting last night's poem to good use, equating the inner workings of my brain that should definitely be relegated to the privacy of a diary with prose from which the entire student body could benefit.

Dear Editor,
I would like to submit a poem/paragraph of creative
writing to the school newspaper. It is called Mr. He

and I have attached it to this email. I would be very grateful if you published it.

Sincerely,
Marissa Miller, Secondary 2

He walks through the halls like the king of the world, but really, he's just an old skater kid. He's got tons of friends and is wayy liked. But no one likes him as much as me, of course. Sometimes he gets bored during class so he sends me cute emails, or sneaks into the bathroom to call me. Naughty skater boys like him do that kinda thing. He wouldn't call me hot, or remind me that my tits are out of this world. He calls me sweetheart, beautiful, and darling. We hold hands and make out in parks until it's dark and soon enough we're fooling around under the moon-lit sky. He'll make me laugh, and look irresistible when he plays guitar or some sort of physical activity. He also has nice lips, really soft also. He thinks I'm hysterical, but doesn't laugh at every single one of my jokes. He takes the time to tell me how special I am, and starts to blush like mad. But I find it cute nonetheless. We have so much in common that it gets scary. We sit there gazing into each other's eyes that we start feeling butterflies in our stomachs until we just can't take the anticipation any longer. Sometimes we talk about life, and how drugs are bad. He promised me he wouldn't cheat, and kept his word. He's a tough guy, I mean, every single girl wants a piece of him. He also assures me that my hair looks better naturally curly. He doesn't think it's

weird when I use big words, because he does so himself. He
finds these really sweet ways to say he loves me, because he
means it with all his heart. Man, he was the best idea I've
ever had.

The week after sending that email, I removed my headphones once I saw a group of boys walking toward me in
the hallway, their lips moving animatedly.

"Can I help you?" I asked, looking up at a swath of
surfer hair heads and low-slung baggy pants.

"Well, which one of us is it?" asked a boy from two
grades above me. He loomed over me so closely I could
smell the cafeteria chocolate chip cookies on his breath.

"Which one of you is what?" I replied, confused.

"He. Which one of us is Mr. He?" said another.

"Yeah, I have soft lips. See?" another one chimed in
from the back, mimicking a duck face you'd make when
posing for a selfie. I had no idea what they were talking
about.

Until I did.

I wished I could take it all back. This wasn't supposed
to happen. All I wanted was to blend in, to continue to be
comfortably invisible. The kids at recess once basically
held a democratic election to allow me to be their friend—
there was no way I could afford to give them any reason to
change their mind and impeach me from their group. Now,
these boys were probably all imagining me getting fondled
on a park bench. That was so not the plan. I wanted to use
writing as a silent way to express myself without stuttering

through a speech to a crowd, confronting an enemy, or admitting I was in love. No one fucking read the school newspaper. Why did they have to start now?

"Yo, leave this poor kid alone," Gordon said, lowering his voice to his friends. A two-year age gap was a lot back then.

"They're just being dicks. Ignore them," he said, motioning toward me. I never meant to be friends with him in the first place, but he lived a couple blocks away from me, so I associated him with the concept of home. We would run into each other during afternoon bike rides going in the same direction and stop for Tim Horton's iced cappuccinos on the way, pausing only to sip them while staring at the clouds on a pair of creaky swings. There was a mutual understanding that we had so little in common there was no expectation to converse, like a silent poem. That made it easy.

With a knowing glance at his friends, Gordon led me away from the heckling hooligans who were now chanting "Mr. He! Mr. He!"

"Look, dude. You're really smart and a good writer," he continued. "They're just poking fun."

"I don't get it. If I was that good, they wouldn't have bothered me like that," I said.

They weren't so much mocking the act of writing itself. They were making fun of me. Thinking back on it, yeah, I made myself a target. In that single clumsy paragraph, I encapsulated how deeply my self-worth hinged on loving and being loved. I used specific language to describe arousal and attraction. I asserted my dating likes and dislikes. Either they were threatened by my pseudo-confidence and wanted me to feel as low as they did, or they figured only someone easy would call attention to her "tits" in the school newspaper. The attacks felt personal, because the poem was very much emblematic of who I was: a thirteen-year-old feminist, or whatever you want to call it, who didn't know there was anything wrong with wanting to be wanted.

Only now, I was perpetually ashamed of it.

Our bike rides intersected at the park closest to his house two weeks later. By then, some of the shame had worn off. Gordon and I had a lot more to talk about on the swings this time around, what with his swooping-in-to-save-the-day big brother move.

"I see something in you that they don't," he said, resting his elbows on his knees. "You're not like the other biddies."

It was poetry to my ears. Everyone wants to hear they're "not like other biddies," yet still be treated as if they fit right in.

"There are a lot more poems where that came from. If you promise not to judge, I can show you more," I said.

"I would be honored. Until then, wanna come in? Looks like it might rain," he said, squinting up at a slate-gray sky.

"Sure, why not," I said, walking my bike into his parents' garage. He protected me—of course I felt safe hanging out with someone who positioned himself as the brother I never had.

Even though his family had moved in fifteen years prior, his basement was unfinished. I sat cross-legged on the green couch to avoid splinters on my soles, and asked him to decode a text from one of my six crushes. I plucked a faux-fur throw from behind me and parachuted it over my body.

"Oh, he defs likes you. No question about it," Gordon said definitively. "The fact that he said 'ttyl' with a smiley emoticon means that he wasn't saying he'll talk to you later to end the conversation, but because he actually had to go and can't wait to talk to you again. Guys don't use emoticons unless they're thinkin' marriage." My chest swelled with relief. Surely, this older guy knew what he was talking about.

It was still pouring rain outside, and I wasn't about to topple over face-first into a puddle on my bike ride home, so I stuck it out a bit longer.

He decided we'd watch *The O.C.* since I shared the same name as the main character; he fast-forwarded to the episode where Marissa dies.

Before then, I had never sat on a couch with a boy. Only on a bench with an imaginary one from my poem. What were the rules? I didn't want him to get the wrong impression if I looked at him or made comments during the show. To keep my hands occupied, I popped popcorn into my mouth with the ferocity of a carbo-loading marathoner. Ever so slightly, his knee pressed harder into mine. *Fine*, I thought. *I guess this is a pretty small couch.* I uncrossed my legs and folded my arms into my chest to take up less space. I retreated into myself, not knowing who I was when I wasn't imitating Jenna's expansive reach over her desk, or reading a women's magazine that would tell me exactly what to do in this situation. The more he inched closer to me, the harder I felt my ribs dig into the armrest.

I was too preoccupied trying to develop pathos for characters I had never watched to notice what Gordon was doing. Over the barrier of my thick hoodie, his hands traced a line from my elbow crease to the side of my breast where it met my left nipple. That same feeling washed over me as it did when a barricade of his friends ambushed me in the hallway chanting the title of my poem back at me like a spell: panic.

The friction against those delicate nerve endings sent a wave of energy down my spine, but my mind hadn't yet caught up to my body quick enough to react.

He grabbed me by both shoulders and pulled my chest into his. Mid-chew, particles of popcorn exfoliated my palate as his lips shoehorned mine open. I sat there, CPR-dummy motionless.

I gave him a chance. After all, I had recently read in *Cosmo* that researchers have found new language to describe women's arousal. Unlike the spontaneous, on-command desire most men are able to experience, women often get aroused by something called responsive desire in response to or in anticipation of physical touch, as opposed to the actual touch itself. I put that theory into practice, and waited, and waited. Four minutes later, his tongue in my mouth was still a lost slug on a damp sidewalk.

I was more turned on by the idea of him being turned on by me in a dirty hoodie with a mouth full of junk food. But not turned on enough to experience this responsive desire concept *Cosmo* spoke of. Still the Sahara Desert down there.

Everyone knows where they were when Donald Trump was elected president of the United States. I will never forget where I was when I saw my first penis. Why Gordon chose to whip his out during Marissa's funeral scene in *The O.C.* eludes me to this day. Up until then, the only penises I had seen were when I "accidentally" typed "sex" into the search bar on my parents' dial-up internet, leading to fifteen different viruses I pretended weren't my fault.

"Dude!" I shrieked. "Put it away!"

"I thought you wanted it," he said matter-of-factly.

"I don't know what gave you that impression, but now I'm actually scarred for life," I said.

"Well, next time don't go writing poems about hooking up with guys if you don't want any of this," he said, referring to his still-hard penis hanging out of his school uniform gym shorts.

I gathered my belongings and silently tiptoed out of his basement without saying good-bye. The last thing I wanted to do was make a scene, to offend him, or to make him angry. He was older. He was right. I should have wanted him. What was wrong with *me*?

Without a sound, I hopped onto my bike and pedaled as if I were escaping a version of myself I wish I never knew.

Six blocks down and too upset to find my keys, I rang my parents' doorbell teary-eyed. They didn't have to know about the penis. That was all my fault. My mom scooped me into her arms.

"What's wrong, my love?"

"I fell off my bike and scraped my elbow," I said,

running into the shower before she could see my immaculately clean sleeves.

* * *

My grade ten physics exam was in less than a week. I needed a game plan. Fast. I imagined driving off a cliff to exempt myself. No need for a doctor's note when you're dead.

For previous tests, my teacher Gerald Steinberg had given me a mark of six out of ten on examples I left blank. This was a guy who was so afraid to emote in real life that he did so in backhanded, paper-grading ways. He didn't have the emotional faculties to deal with my after-class hysteria, let alone have me fail and retake his class. Giving me grades I didn't deserve wasn't so much an act of charity as it was a strategy to get me the hell away from his office hours.

For that entire week, my mom, a scientist, spent her off-hours rotating between TMZ reruns and teaching me material she had learned in Mr. Steinberg's class thirty years prior. The Lancôme Trésor perfume that she wore to work seeped into my nostrils as she taught me. With each homeschooled science lesson, I was closer to the daughter I thought she always wanted me to be.

I was ashamed by my lack of ability to grasp basic concepts, but as his former student, my mom knew just how little patience Mr. Steinberg had for students who didn't "get it" on their first try—or in my case, specifically, students who drew dicks with varying degrees of hairiness in their notebook atop each parabola like a scepter. They made

Jenna roll her eyes the way lunch monitors do when "boys are just being boys."

"It amazes me how you find a new way to make me vomit every day," Jenna once said, glancing over at my notebook on a day when my subject of choice was particularly veiny.

My friendship with Jenna began at age eight when she raised her hand in the schoolyard, allowing me to play Blue's Clues. It didn't quite occur to me that most friendships don't undergo (pardon the double negative) a democratic screening process. Cool girls who wore their hair in all the right ways were born with the power to veto me out of their lives like an unconstitutional bill. This was my normal. Wasn't it everyone's?

What marked our friendship was after-school Dairy Queen runs and visions of Jenna watching in horror as I made Barbie and Ken enact Kama Sutra positions. Every class we had taken together since, Jenna would shift her entire eighty pounds of weight into her forearms and onto the page while engrossed in a math problem, often spilling her bony elbows onto my desk. She took up space in a way I could never fathom. I had never allowed myself to spill into something so publicly, so fully. But seeing her do it inspired me to lean into my desk, too. A performance. You are socialized to assimilate in the elementary school's ecosystem, conforming to the pack mentality your only road to survival. The idea that opposites might attract is not yet part of your lexicon. It's all "Play with the same Barbies or bust."

I ended up in physics with her for that same reason. If I wanted to fit in, I could take physics, chemistry, and a slew of other courses that elevated my blood pressure just by thinking about them; if I wanted to stick out like a sore writer's callused middle finger, I could take creative writing and work on my poems. I shuddered to think about what had happened to me the first time I let a poem out into the world.

Mr. He! Mr. He! Mr. He!

I found solace in the way math concretely determined success. You either got an A, or you didn't. With writing, my work either invited Facebook likes or nonconsensual penis appearances. I couldn't stand the uncertainty of how my audience would receive me. After all, writing wasn't just words on a page. It was me.

I sat with Jenna in physics, her torso enveloping me as she Sheryl Sandberg–Leaned In to the page. God forbid I deviated from our unspoken friendship vows solidified over soft-serve and Barbies, let alone disappointed my parents who spoke math as a first language. Having her in class with me was my Freudian transitional object easing me into unfamiliar territory, the same way a child clings to a teddy bear well into adolescence as a reminder of their mother.

I left the class with nothing to show for it but a bouquet of expertly shaded penises. The following morning, I asked my mom to buy me one of those expensive two-hundred-page physics crash courses. I could no longer absorb information in the presence of other people. Parents (at home) and crushes (at school) were mirrors through which I could see how inadequate, inferior, and incapable I was. It would be far more productive if I could be terrible within the confines of my own solitude. Two hundred pages later, I finally had some semblance of an idea of what I was doing.

Before I sat down at my desk in the auditorium to take the exam, I gave my stomach a pep talk.

Look, buddy. No fucked-up noises this time. No one needs to know you put five Splendas in your coffee this morning and ate a bowl of flax. Everyone thinks you're weird enough as it is. Please, keep your literal shit together, I said in my head.

The panic set in. My skin turned hot as I scanned each page of the exam. I scribbled down what I could, harkening back to my hovering mom, the Lancôme perfume, and Jenna's leaning on the desk.

For once in my life I wasn't about to cry, so I found it weird that my nose was runny. I swiped a finger across my nostrils, noticing a faint tickle. I froze. I had unlocked a faucet of blood. I wondered if I should get up and leave a crimson Hansel and Gretel trail behind me as I searched for Kleenex with my arms extended in front of me like Frankenstein, or watch the blood travel at a velocity of twenty feet per second over a distance of two feet as it landed on the third page of my exam.

"Leave the room," Mr. Steinberg said, making my decision for me. My cheeks were as red as the trail I left in my wake.

In the bathroom, I spent the next forty-five minutes with my head tilted back ninety degrees, dizzy from both a loss of blood and what remaining amount of it I now had traveling toward my head. That moment confirmed my suspicions: my biggest fear wouldn't be returning to the menacing school hallways as a born-again poet but breaking the news to my parents that I'd rather bleed out in a public bathroom until someone finds my decomposed body than solve another math problem.

* * *

If I didn't do it now, I never would.

My dad sat at the kitchen table mixing ghost pepper hot sauce into his coffee. "It's supposed to speed up metabolism," he once said. My mom was rolling more *knish* dough between her palms in preparation for an early fall Rosh Hashanah. It was June.

"Mom, Dad, there's something I need to tell you," I said. My teeth chattered against the ceramic mug as I took a sip of coffee.

"We're listening," my mom said.

"As you know, everything I do in life is to make you proud of me. I can't make a single decision without your input because I'm so afraid of disappointing you," I began. "I know I said I wanted to be a brain surgeon and you were all in favor of that, but I think the real reason why is because it would be an opportunity to look at gross things all day. I can barely solve the displacement of a truck if it's traveling at three meters per second squared for three minutes. How am I going to perform a craniotomy without checking the user manual and taking nervous pee breaks every ten minutes? It is with a heavy heart and a nervous brain that I am telling you I'm g—"

"Marissa, we know," they said in unison. "We know you're going into journalism."

"But it was my best-kept secret," I said.

"You hide a lot of things, but a parent always knows," my mom said.

Had they overheard my conversation with an ex who told me I'd be a ten if only I went into journalism, knowing full well a man's opinion of me trumps any sort of satisfaction I'd derive out of an endeavor that spoke to me anyway? Or was it my budding interest in speaking out against injustices and giving the voiceless a safe place to tell their truths?

I thought about all the fake bruised elbows, the lighters they found that fell out of my jean pockets into the washing machine, the carton of cigarettes tucked into my school bag, the condom that fell out of my boyfriend's pocket while we were at the family dinner table because we were playing some perverted iteration of "dress-up" with it and it couldn't go in the garbage for all to see. Having my parents catch me in those lies felt infinitely more traumatic than what I had just revealed. Here, writing was not a choice. It was an identity.

The relief felt anticlimactic. I had prepared for a fight of apocalyptic proportions. What good did it serve to anticipate the worst? I could have devoted all that mental energy to actually writing instead of hiding in my closet with all my contraband weed paraphernalia.

I left the house before they could change their minds about me.

"Guys, you won't believe what just happened," I breathlessly said to my friends as I got into the car.

Jenna was perched on her boyfriend Tim's lap, even though there was space for both of them to sit side by side. Tim was playing a silent game of "Chicken or Go" with her upper thigh. In the passenger seat, Oliver flipped through his iPod Nano so quickly it sounded like we were driving through a tunnel. In the driver's seat, Sam held one hand on the wheel and one fist in the air to greet mine.

"My parents were literally so cool with me crushing their dreams of me being a doctor. I basically told them to fuck off in a very polite way," I said, trying to sound nonchalant as a way to undermine just how powerful of a moment I shared with them minutes before.

"Your parents are chill. I had no doubt about it," Oliver said without looking up from his iPod.

Sam's prehistoric Corolla hobbled along the highway until we pulled up to the backyard party at our friend Michaela's. I felt acutely aware of my empty hands as I watched everyone else at the party double fist this, smoke that. Sam and Oliver came up from behind Jenna and me with a tray of shots.

"Ladies? One for you, one for you, and two for us," Oliver said. Sips of Jack Daniels sank down my esophagus in bullets. Poison.

"Hey, that reminds me," Sam said. "Know how you basically just came out to your parents that you want to be a struggling artist? I have a friend of a friend who actually does that, minus the struggling part. I think he's here. One sec," Sam trailed off gesticulating maniacally.

Had I not felt the whiskey travel straight to my brain, I would have shuddered at the thought of meeting someone new, someone probably older and wiser and better than me in every regard. Someone with the foresight to see through my bullshit.

A couple minutes later, a man with a dark gaze and head of hair approached me without saying a word. I was at eye level with the chest hair poking out of his white V-neck T-shirt.

"Oh, hi," I said. "Sam's friend?"

He shook my hand while frowning, but not in a mean way. He was just several years older, and when you're older, it takes a lot more to impress you, I thought.

"He tells me you're a writer, huh," he said. It wasn't quite a question or a statement, so I wasn't sure how to respond.

Up until that point, my writing had been confined to my MySpace blog and the margins of my notebooks. I could be a Pulitzer Prize deep into my career and still have trouble self-identifying as a writer. And I certainly wasn't about to start in the presence of a taller, older man in a V-neck that somehow didn't reek of *Jersey Shore*. If there was anyone that would out me as a fraud, it would be him.

"I've written some poems here and there. Letters to my friends at camp. That sort of thing," I said. I would die of shame if he saw my MySpace.

"Well, if you ever want to give reporting a shot, you know where to find me," V-neck said.

No, I didn't know where to find him. And I never would because he immediately spun around to join a game of beer pong.

A few days later, I received a Facebook friend request from someone with a familiar name. I clicked on the photo, noticing those same dark eyes and that subtle patch of chest hair peeking out from a V-neck T-shirt, or maybe it was a plaid button-down. His communication method of choice intrigued me. It was a wall post that said, "Let's have you write for the paper."

Had this been sometime after 2009 when wall posts became akin to thinly veiled digital marriage proposals, I would have needed an entire week to dissect the message, phone a friend, ask the audience, and schedule an appointment with my therapist before responding. So I did what any reasonable person would do in that situation: I signed out of my account before I could reply with something stupid.

It was time to pack up for work anyways. On my lunch break as a dance teacher, I huddled in front of my laptop drafting cover letters and updating my resume in an attempt to trick the journalism and creative writing departments at Concordia University into accepting me. I felt like a giant, human embodiment of a lie using words to describe myself like "determined, meticulous, and news-loving." I called my then-boyfriend, the one who pregamed my parents' Passover Seder and peed in sinks, to tell him I was applying. As a news junkie with strong opinions on the BBC, he was supposed to be excited. This was supposed to impress him. He was my age, after all.

"Good luck. Don't become part of the problem," he said.

"You have something in the mail," my mom said, handing me a white envelope three months later. I only got mail when organizations I've never heard of asked for donations.

Dear Marissa Miller,
We would like to congratulate you on your acceptance to **Journalism (Major)** and **Creative Writing (Minor)** at Concordia University. We look forward to welcoming you next fall.

My first thought was "Now that I've come out to my parents, what a relief it is to not have to lead a double life by scattering fake chemistry textbooks across the house the way closeted gay men splay posters of half-naked women on their bedroom walls like half the guys I've dated." My second thought was "this has to be a mistake." Had the administration actually read my resume or cover letters, they would have learned I had no place pursuing this writing thing professionally. I mean, I used words like "passion" and "journey" in my cover letter, for fuck's sake. Gag me with a spoon.

What threw me off guard about the acceptance was that I was more familiar with the feeling of rejection. It happened in the schoolyard when I just wanted to play. It happened when my ninth-grade boyfriend dumped me at a concert during "our song." It happened when my English teacher told me to "stop bragging" when I won first place in the country in a poetry competition that *she told me to enter*. It happened when the most popular girl at sleepaway camp kicked me in the stomach and called me a slut because her crush chose me over her.

Feeling lonelier and more fraudulent than I ever had before, I emailed V-neck a week after meeting him to take him up on his offer to write for *The Link*, one of the two school newspapers at Concordia. He asked me to come into his office to discuss story ideas. Look, I'm no expert, but in my experience anxiously scanning message boards and googling "how to write for magazines Cosmopolitan Teen Vogue etc.," I know these exchanges are best kept online. Eye contact is so 2004. And why take notes at an in-person meeting when email leaves a perfectly organized paper trail?

I put on a blouse that I sweat through wet T-shirt contest–style on the bus on the way to his office downtown because I was so nervous. The newsroom looked like a cross between a construction site and an abandoned recording studio. Unfinished wooden tables lined the perimeter of the office. Splatters of paint coated orange plastic chairs. Front pages of the paper replaced actual wallpaper. It was all so gritty and cool—the antithesis of the newsroom depicted in *The Devil Wears Prada* where floor-to-ceiling windows let in so much sunlight you wouldn't dare come into work hungover.

V-neck shook my hand and ushered me into his office. He was what your grandmother would call handsome, which is to say, not at all for me. But he looked so regal behind a desk all I could think about pitching him was sappy prose about the way I wanted him to tear my moist top off of me—if only because my shirt was starting to smell from the anxiety sweat. Those were my surface fantasies. In my heart of hearts, my real fantasy was to find a guy who didn't think it was weird when I used big words, because he did so himself.

But this wasn't about courtship and mating. I was primarily there to try my hand at real journalism and build my portfolio. I was secondarily there to prove to myself I was capable of having a professional and cordial relationship with a member of the opposite sex without the looming threat of a surprise penis appearance during a funeral scene. To be, you know, normal. Not to have this well-adjusted editor menacingly chant "Mr. He! Mr. He!" as he swatted me with a rolled-up newspaper like a fruit fly out of his office.

My dad was more excited about the pitch meeting than I was because he felt like he could participate. He was always dreaming up novel ways to relate to me since he never had a son he could take to baseball practice. We ran through his list of clients who'd be at my beck and call in case I needed sources from a variety of industries. "Just tell them you're Sheldon Miller's daughter," he said triumphantly.

I was proud to have him as my dad the way most little sisters brag about their cool older brothers. My dad was the neighborhood mascot. It didn't matter who you were—he was rooting for you, and he would tell you to your face how great you were doing. He didn't believe in formalities. Watching him tell strangers about his weight and irritable bowel disease flareups with such candor is the reason my social cues are not fully developed.

Did I want to interview a model? my dad suggested. Not serious enough. A lawyer? Too boring. Finally, we landed on a farmer. V-neck agreed to a career profile about this man's efforts to promote sustainable agriculture in the province of Quebec. There was a due date and a proposed word count and everything. Everyone remembers where they were when they saw their first penis, and where they were when they were assigned their first piece of journalism.

I conducted a painstaking three-hour interview, my questions scribbled on a napkin in front of me. It was a crash course on soil, weather, renewable energy, crops, and cattle. Despite my unfamiliarity with the topic, it was practice for all the academic and (maybe one day) professional articles I'd be assigned. As much as I would have loved to be a beat reporter, I'd be limiting my opportunities if I clung to one idea in hopes that the news neatly fit into it. The world happens whether you like it or not. I was ready to show my Journalism God—some dude in green Converse sneakers with chest hair peeking out from under his V-neck—that I was capable of writing about ideas outside my own insignificant suburban world.

I felt like less of an embarrassment as a human being a month later as I filed a piece of journalism that had nothing to do with kissing, calories, and sports bras—topics that I was no longer allowed to admit I cared about on a profound, existential level lest I be chased down the hallways by a loud herd of bros with surfer hair.

"This is good," he wrote back. "But we need to name your source."

"He wants to go anonymous," I said.

"There needs to be a pressing reason why we can't reveal his identity, safety being one of them."

"Oh, it's nothing like that," I said. "He's just never been interviewed before and isn't sure if I'll make him sound good."

It wasn't my job to make him "sound good." My job was to relay what he said in an unbiased fashion, and to tell his story without upselling it to the reader. I pat myself on the back for getting at least one thing right. One week deep into my journalism degree, we were still covering basic sentence structure. Ethics surrounding anonymous sources were a couple months away in the class syllabus. But I wasn't about to wait for a man on a podium to talk at me about journalism. I had to do it off the clock. Even if it looked messy as hell.

"If he's not going to let us name him, we'll have to kill the piece," V-neck said in his final email.

Kill. Murder. Death. He tossed around this journalism jargon like a Frisbee in a grassy field, its finality numbing. I could have interviewed more sources to revive the piece, but I was so embarrassed about committing such an elementary mistake that I refused to work with V-neck ever again.

My disappointment was overshadowed only by the familiar comfort of failure. It enveloped me like a heavy crocheted quilt in front of a fire. Failing meant I could only get better from there, which I'd proved to myself, to my parents, and to my teachers time and time again. I could always learn how and when to name my sources properly, the same way I learned that it's okay to think of math as a bunch of calories working together in different ways, if that's what it takes to wrap my head around it. Had I not made those errors then, I would have made them when the stakes were a lot higher.

There was still that nagging feeling that my mom would pop out of a bush somewhere and say, "Told you so!" I wasn't worried she'd debase me for blowing my first writing assignment—I was worried I would worry her, that she'd fear for my entire future, that this one audition determined the trajectory of my entire life. She had a habit of claiming my problems as her own in an act of solidarity, which would have been sweet had she not catastrophized the extent to which certain incidents caused me pain. Her worry often added a layer of anxiety on top of whatever existed inside of me. It's not like she—or anyone, for that matter—could possibly understand why failure was the only road to success—writing and otherwise.

A month later, I became an editor at the competing school newspaper. It's where I learned that being able to constantly anticipate the worst is the cornerstone of surviving in journalism. It's precisely what made me cut out for it. Stories fall through. Sources cancel. Editors ghost. Pitches end up in the trash. In fearing my parents would be disappointed with my career choice, I was inadvertently flexing my most important professional muscle.

I silenced the part of my brain that reveled in the revenge against V-neck, and celebrated the part of my body that leaned into the page like Jenna as I edited and wrote about kissing, calories, and sports bras. It may not have been Pulitzer Prize material, but it was the opportunity to write in and of itself that was the greatest victory of all.

Chapter 4

JEW CAMP

My parents shipped me off to camp every summer for several years. Instead of having anxiety at home, I could have anxiety at a sleepaway camp an hour and a half away. Having survived the ripped bathing suit saga, I graduated from day camp and was expected to Be Okay in the wilderness north of Montreal. I didn't want to be anxious—what could be better than a month-long sleepover with all your pals, doing each other's nails and borrowing each other's frilly tops? I told myself that if I just tried all the things that normal kids liked, my brain would catch up with my body, like when you smile when you're sad and magically feel happy again.

I finally agreed to go to camp after my best friend Diana took me on a walk around her neighborhood in Côte Saint-Luc and hyped me up.

"You don't understand—there are cookies all the time," she said. "And activities you've never done before like archery and sailing, which I know for a fact you haven't done because I know your whole life."

This wasn't her first rodeo. She had been attending the camp since Rocky Point, the age group so young staff are prepared to perform diaper changes. She was like me in that it wasn't uncommon for her to pick at a random orifice midconversation. She was also like me in that we coauthored a sex ed book for teenage girls using glitter, crayons, and silly putty when we were ten years old and called it "Don't Worry About It" ("Everyone either has a dick or vagina or none or both. There's nothing to be ashamed of! Don't worry about it!"). If she could exist as the only "weirdo" at camp and survive multiple summers surrounded by Jewish Canadian Princesses, surely, I'd thrive with her by my side.

The day before camp, we assembled in the park with our other best friend Jenna (at age eleven, everyone is your best friend if they share their Legos, but these were my actual best friends because they were cool with period stuff). Even though sections were segregated by gender, we needed a game plan as to how we would stalk our collective crush Todd. He had the biggest head any of us had ever seen, and somehow that translated to him probably having cool thoughts up there. "Hopefully they're about me," we cooed.

We kissed our moms and dads good-bye and said hello to the summertime. On a yellow school bus, I instinctively grabbed a seat two spots behind Todd because even then I knew how to play the game. Diana and Jenna fought to sit right behind him. Weak move. I personally would not have gone with that. "It's okay, guys, you can turn around to talk to me so he doesn't think you're stalking him," I said in an effort to be their Designated Cool Female.

After forty-five minutes of staring at the back of Todd's gargantuan head, I suddenly saw it shift and turn toward the window. *What a beautiful, pensive profile*, I thought. He's probably not talking to me because he's busy daydreaming about me.

He proceeded to lift the sliding window, creating a slit of air that blew a slit of fresh countryside breeze onto my face. Closing my eyes, I relished in it. It got me excited about archery and sailing and whatever else they'd throw us kids into to prevent us from beating the living shit out of each other. Once he stuck his massive head out the window (OMG, we have so much in common—we both like fresh air!), he proceeded to lurch himself forward. His eyeballs theatrically popped out of his impressive cranium and he unleashed a stream of pink chunks that splattered a strawberry shortcake-esque batter onto the windows behind it. Luckily, my window was closed, but it drifted by me like liquid from a paintball gun and splattered onto campers behind me. Despite my phobia of vomit, all I could think about what just happened was, *Wow, this is as close as I will get to seeing what the contents of his big brain look like.* And that, friends, was my first brush with true love.

* * *

I was thrilled to be in bunk five, because it was the first cabin in my unit closest to the volleyball net. The volleyball net is where the boys populated to play volleyball, and where the girls, similarly, congregated to play "volleyball." Diana, Jenna, and I had one goal for the summer, and one goal only: to get Todd to like us. Naturally, when we saw his large head bobbing up and down with the cadence of his volleyball two weeks into camp, we happened to show up at the right time with our Soffe shorts rolled down just enough to cover our labia. If he didn't notice us as we were—in baggy sweats and too-big hoodies—clearly we had to switch it up.

We didn't discuss what would happen if he chose one of us and not the other, none of us, or two of us. Though Diana and I had been oddly progressive in our pursuit to quell fellow kids about their insecurities surrounding their bodies and private parts, we hadn't gotten to the part of our glittery sex ed book when we discussed how to navigate polyamory. I was fairly confident that because I was cool enough to not sit right behind Todd on the bus, or that I didn't throw a shoe at his large cranium when he vomited, I was ripe for the picking like a juicy Georgia peach.

We weren't going to actually play volleyball. Who do you think we are? Instead, we did what any self-respecting preteen would do. We lay down on the grass, asses up, looking out onto the water as they played ball behind us, peeking over our shoulders every so often to make sure he was looking. He never was. As far as we knew, he didn't even know we were there. Forty-five minutes into lying down idly, I was starting to be over it. I was itchy in all the wrong places and felt a general sense of unease. It was not yet in my lexicon that scratches shouldn't be itched. No one yet taught me any summer camp survival strategies, like slapping your itch with an open palm, or pressing your nails into the itch in the shape of an X.

"Girls, you have ninety minutes before the dance. I repeat, ninety minutes before the dance," our unit head Alyssa shouted from the rec hall. Without even making eye contact with Todd, we bolted to our cabin and undressed for the shower. Dances were a Big. Fucking. Deal. Boys and girls didn't have to "accidentally" show up to the same place at the same time like we did on the volleyball court. It was almost too easy. Our counselors placed us all in a gym converted into a dance floor and expected us to fend for ourselves. But I couldn't even see five feet in front of me through that thick smog of sexual tension in the air.

Two girls in our bunk were already half an hour deep into their Garnier Fructis haircare routine, so we had lots of catching up to do. I gathered my shower caddy and proceeded to hike up the hill, slipping in and out of my cheap Old Navy flip-flops. Yikes, did not enjoy having that twig penetrate the heel of my foot balls-deep. But onward. I had a crush to get hygienic for.

Showering at camp was always a Thing. We wanted to avoid both revealing our naked, growing bodies to our fellow campers and touching the shower curtain that probably had sixty years' worth of funky camp germs caked onto it. Because I was not about to risk having any more cooties than I already did, Diana and Jenna made a human wall around me as I showered with the curtain open.

"Um, Rissy, there's something . . . " Diana said.

"Yeah, I know, I missed a spot," I said, flipping my hair to the side to rinse out that extra bubbly Herbal Essences shampoo.

"No, here," she said, pointing to her rear.

I looked down and shrieked as if a spider had landed on the drain (which was not uncommon in camp showers). Two welts the diameter of baseballs occupied the lower half of both of my ass cheeks. A wine-red ring surrounded a glowing golden mound of pus. I ran out of the shower without having cleaned the rest of my body, limped down the hill (hello, twig up my heel, my old friend), and sat on my bed to cry. Oh, cool. I couldn't sit *or* walk. The plot thickens!

Normally, I would have asked another girl in my bunk to borrow something cute for the dance, like a floral sundress or a flirty skirt. But I knew better than to infect my fellow bunkmates with whatever the hell was going on down there. So I slipped into those same Soffe shorts I wore playing "volleyball," skipping underwear this time so as not to asphyxiate my boils even further.

Diana, Jenna, and I huddled close to each other as we entered the dance, our eyes searching left and right for a large head sticking out of the crowd.

"Hey, Marissa," Todd said. "What's up? I hope we're on the same color war team tomorrow."

Oh great, he notices me the day I catch an actual Passover plague.

"Hi! Yeah, should be really fun!" I looked at Jenna and Diana for approval, both because I needed confirmation that what I said was cool enough, and permission to actually talk to him.

Midconversation, I was starting to feel an unbearable heat coat my entire body. I ran to my counselor and told her I needed to go to the infirmary.

"But I want to go alone. No one can know what happened," I said.

Of course, that wish was not granted, and she accompanied me the whole six-minute walk down the main gravel road. The nurse took one look at my boils and twiggy foot and put her hand over her chest in a way a Jewish mother would when you bring home a *goy*. She placed me on the examination table and told me to disrobe. The courteous thing to do would have been to lie down on my back so as to emotionally prepare the doctor for what she was about to see when she walked into her office. Face down, boils up was all I had the energy for.

"Oh no, honey," she said. The patient-physician alliance was a little different at camp. Pet names were a thing I assumed she was allowed to use so it would help us acclimate to an environment away from our parents. "How did this happen?"

"I was playing volleyball and just started getting itchy, and then a branch got stuck under my foot, and then I tried to take it out because I had to shower, and then I sat down but I couldn't, so I stood until we went to the dance on my half-twiggy foot, and the whole time I was standing I was scratching so hard I could feel my bones," I said.

"It's definitely some sort of bug bite, and my gosh, looks like there's still some branch stuck under your foot. And this happened how long ago?"

"Maybe around six hours," I said.

"Six hours of pain like this, and you only thought to come see me now?"

I instantly wanted to retort that I had a dance to get to, a boy to flirt with, and cookies to stare at but not eat. Instead I just shrugged and gave her another excuse that wasn't totally a lie.

"I don't know," I said. "I didn't want to bother you in case you had other more important stuff going on."

"That's what I'm here for. It's my job to help you. Never be shy to put your health first," she said.

I didn't see it as a health matter because I didn't have a cold or a fever. And at age eleven, I only considered myself sick if my digestive and respiratory systems were compromised. That is: tummy ache and sniffles. Preferably with the symptom of decreased appetite. That was always a bonus.

After putting on a pair of rubber gloves, the camp doctor proceeded to press down on each side of my infected bug bites. Small droplets of liquid leaked onto a gauze pad. After about five minutes of gently pressing down on the perimeter of my left abscess, thicker blobs not unlike melted butter projectile flew out of its now-bleeding crater. I was flexible enough to see what was going on, so I took advantage of the front row seat to *Trauma: Life in the ER:* Jew Camp edition.

My foot was out of commission for the next day, so I could forget about being on Big Head's color war team.

It was the bluest my lady balls had ever been.

But luckily, I had each year at camp after that to explore my sexuality. I lost so much time to getting the pus and blood sucked out of various holes when I could have been flirting.

I flirted by being very into things guys were interested in. Campers weren't allowed phones, so naturally, nudie mags trickled into duffle bags sandwiched between big sweaters. I always managed to hang out in boys' cabins and tents because of how well I blended in—outside their tents, you could hear my loud and raspy voice hollering about tampons, which I affectionately referred to as "cunt cloggers." There's no way a nice Jewish girl would talk like that while Hashem was listening.

I listened to them strum along to predictable camp classics from bands like Oasis, Green Day, and Coldplay, always sitting across from them on empty milk crates and toolboxes, and never on their beds. My T-shirts were not unlike theirs—loose-fitting, ripped around the armpits, and boasting bands either no one's heard of or everyone was sick to death of. It thus, from what I can deduce, felt like a safe enough environment for them to be themselves around me. To be boys.

One Saturday on Shabbat when the whole camp was quiet, I was sitting in a tent in my unit called The Village with three boys, Gordon, Max, and Brent. They all went to school with each other but never made me feel left out because of it. I became the honorary fourth bro in their circle, because not only did I put up with their poop jokes but I contributed to, provoked, and ranked them in order of weakest to strongest, extending equal weight to both structure and delivery. Since no activities were ever scheduled on Saturday—what with us being prohibited from using electricity and carrying anything, for example—we were free to reflect on all the sins we committed that week and how we could do better the following one (well, the former is technically what we do at post-Shabbat *Havdallah* services). My sin that week was probably shitting in the woods somewhere, so I kind of half-heartedly said sorry to the sky when it came time for us to stand around a beeswax candle that smelled of spicy *besamim*.

The forced spirituality of Shabbat incited an almost Neanderthal-like mischievous streak in all of us. Once the boys' fingers were (quite literally) all strung out from their seventh go at Bittersweet Symphony, they collapsed onto their beds while I sat in comfortable silence. Gordon matter-of-factly pulled a *Hustler* magazine out from under his thin pillow like the tooth fairy left it there for him to savor while his bunkmates were on another planet.

"My dad said if I want to become a man, I need to start looking at these," he said without an ounce of contempt in his voice. I saw a glimpse of the model's bronzed body through the glare of sun cutting through the mosquito net–covered window. You could have served charcuterie off the model's abs. I didn't recognize her, but she was some type of Jessica Alba–Jessica Simpson hybrid. Like me reading women's magazines as a Bible (you're welcome, Hashem), Gordon was ready and willing to commit to the literature. His own Sherpa up the hill. As a woman (or rather a fifteen-year-old girl), I had magazines telling me how to look, act, and feel. As a man (or rather a sixteen-year-old boy), he had magazines telling him who to fuck and what they should look like.

Gordon passed the magazine around to his, our, two friends Brent and Max, hurling simulations of cat-calls at the inanimate page. They didn't even pretend to come off as having been there before. Upon squinting their eyes to get a better view, all three of them placed pillows over their laps.

"Can I see it, too?" I asked.

They all looked up at me, stunned that I wasn't shunning them for looking at a naked woman—on God's holiest day of the week, no less. I wasn't even trying to be that fake chill girl who's deep down seething and upset. I genuinely wanted to see what the fuss was about.

It wasn't so much her body itself that fascinated me—although it did instill a pang of insecurity—it was her complete and utter release of inhibition. I wondered what it felt like to live in a world where showing a sliver of nipple was considered as normal as, say, flaunting your shoulders at the beach but not quite in synagogue.

They looked at me looking at the magazine, unable to fathom the idea of a woman being on board with porn.

"Damn, I wish I could do that," I said.

Six eyebrows lifted a full inch up their foreheads.

"I mean, not like *that* that. More like be naked and okay with my body as a thing that exists as both a vehicle of pleasure and one that carries around our organs and is capable of love and digestion and isn't the enemy but the thing we are nothing without," I said.

"Bro," Max said.

"I know," I replied.

"No need to get all Gandhi on us, dude," Brent chimed in. I stood up off the empty red milk crate and paced back and forth.

"I just have this feeling that, like, maybe looking at other people celebrating their bodies can help me celebrate mine? Like maybe I hate my love handles so much because I've quite literally never seen any others in the flesh besides those awkward five minutes in the changing room after gym class? Like, I'm looking at this person's naked body way more in awe than I should be. It's a body. It's nothing to worship, and it's nothing to denigrate. If I saw more bodies in my life, maybe I wouldn't have these unmanageable feelings of disdain for my own and wild obsession with others," I said, breathless and excited about my revelation.

I kissed all three of them that summer to find out if I was gay. Turns out I just wasn't into my friends that way.

* * *

I do this thing where I develop massive crushes on all my gay editors. The crushes are both a product of finding them genuinely attractive, interesting, and smart, and being jealous they're living their truth. Professionally, my crushes tend to work to my advantage. They force me to work extra hard in crafting and perfecting my pitches and reported stories, and they encourage me to try a little harder in looking hot on social media. Not that it matters because they aren't into women.

In 2014, one such editor worked at a major online news outlet and agreed to take me on as a writer. He was constantly flaky and treated me like shit, but I loved him for it (because being treated like shit was all I knew, LOL). I had spent weeks and weeks studying his social media presence to determine what he liked on a personal level. I was always under the suspicion that, regardless of a media outlet's mandate or political leanings, certain editors were more likely to commission stories in which they had a vested interest. I considered this to ring especially true for lifestyle topics, as opposed to breaking news.

I was thrilled to learn that after hours of stalking, he was interested in the culture of porn, the same way I was. I thought about porn stars as people with parents and children and pets, and while I was certainly interested in earning $250 in US currency off each story, my goal was mostly to impress him.

Our initial pitch phone call was scheduled for a Monday (there must be a target on my forehead that reads, "Let's put on our professional voices for a hot sec and judge each other while we speak."). The conversation felt so smooth I consciously told myself to stop flirting. I told him what I wanted to write about, and he assigned several stories on the spot. It was hot, as if I would get an allowance for doing the chore of being his good little journalist.

A handful of my pieces got killed because he changed jobs before they could get published, and the new editor had "no bandwidth" to take them on. But a couple important stories did fall through the cracks and get published. One of them was a piece on moms in porn. I interviewed a handful about how they reconcile their two identities as porn stars and moms. Nothing groundbreaking, but exciting to report on nonetheless.

Around six years later, I got a Twitter DM from someone claiming to be the son of a porn star. He had read my piece. That could only mean two things, because there are only two camps of reader mail: the first type wants me fucking dead because I misplaced a comma and am "left-wing trash," and the second type wants to let me know how much my piece resonated with them. Travis came from neither camp, so I had no idea what to do with him. I kept an open mind and just let him talk.

He began by first thanking me for writing the article on moms in porn. Standard stuff. I usually don't engage much further with fans past "Thanks so much for your feedback!" or "I'm so glad it helped you!" But this guy, as they say on *Silicon Valley*, this guy fucks.

Or at least his mom does.

He then began opening up to me about getting bullied every day at school in his teenage years. His classmates would constantly tell him how they jerked off to his mom the night before, and sometimes filmed themselves doing it. He even went so far as to send me a video of himself crying to a link of his mom getting railed by some oily buff guy she met online. My initial reaction was to be shocked because that's how "society" expects me to respond to a dynamic as unusual as the one I was being confronted with. But after all, his mother, who happened to be a porn star, like anyone, like all of us, had parents and children and pets.

Travis continued to send me several paragraphs upon paragraphs of DMs per day, each of them more heartbreaking than the last. Sometimes he would be typing to me from his bedroom while trying to block his ears to the sound of his mother having loud sex in the next room over. I felt conflicted breaching the unwritten writer/reader boundary rule I made up in my head that physicians practice with patients. I would respond curtly, but I always responded.

"Just put on some headphones and listen to a podcast or an album," I suggested one night when he said the sound of the headboard hitting the wall was particularly deafening.

"I can't believe you just said that," he said.

"Excuse me?" I replied.

"I'm shocked," he continued, unhelpfully.

Okay, I lied. This is where I got frustrated and left him on "read".

"I mean, any time I confide in someone about living with my mom who's a porn star, they start apologizing and feeling sorry for me and making it weird," he said. "You just treat me like a normal person."

"Because you are a normal person," I said.

He told me no one had ever validated him like that. Not even his therapist. And while my suspicion was correct—engaging with him did, in fact, provoke him to borderline stalk me—I don't regret telling him that he is okay, he is not a bad person, and that he doesn't deserve to be in pain. I ignored my privilege of coming from a family of scientists and accountants and thought about what it must be like to be thrust into circumstances that are both beyond his control and anyone's comprehension.

When he told me he preferred talking to me over his therapist, I knew it was time to cut the cord. I blocked him, but not out of malice or spite. My goal was for him to take what he learned from our conversations—the self-worth, the validation—and begin to internalize it. I couldn't sustain myself any longer operating as a vending machine of support. It drained me. The same way it probably drained others to lift me up when I didn't have the energy to do it myself.

Two months after blocking him, I got an email from him that read:

Hi Marissa,
Good Afternoon! It's Travis (the one who's mom is a pornstar)....I'm sorry I forced you to block me back in June. You had every right to. I didn't react in the best way. I hope you have been well and maybe we can keep in touch every now and then.
Thank you for your time.

I didn't respond because I had nothing to say. One month after that, he began a new email thread:

Marissa,
Good Morning!!!! Is there any way you could ever forgive me? Do you have Venmo?

I told him I did not have Venmo because it doesn't exist in Canada, and that I also didn't want his money. He then proceeded to ask about any alternatives, like whether he could buy me items from my Amazon wish list, or whether he could purchase any of my books, merch, or workshops.

"No, that's quite alright. I don't want anything from you," I said.

Unable to process what I was saying, he replied: "May I be Your financial bitch boy? You really do have a spell over me." The capitalized Y was very much intentional.

I was startled for a second. The last time I was awarded money I didn't deserve was when my bubby slipped me a twenty dollar bill for not finding the *afikoman*.

Finally, he moved away from the topic of financially supporting me and onto something I could never have been mentally prepared for no matter how many nudie mags I got a glimpse of in a boy's tent, and no matter how many porn-centric articles I wrote for magazines.

"What can I do that can make You smile and laugh? I was thinking first step I could do is give You blackmail," he continued.

I thought about how much dirt I had on him already—
the text chains helping him sleep through the night while his
mother filmed porn in the room over, or the videos of him
weeping to said videos of his mother starring in these films
naked as the day either of them were born.

I felt very uncomfortable engaging in this type of
dynamic with a stranger, but that was only because it was
a role I had never been asked to fulfill before. Yes, he was
absolutely the type of person my parents would have told me
to call the cops on, but I couldn't help but see the humanity
in him. It's reductive—but not wrong—to say our standing
in society often hinges on our families' adherence to socially
acceptable standards and etiquette, and that in this case, he
placed himself squarely in the position of a submissive person because he was never able to participate in this role on
his own terms. He was at the mercy of his mother. This was
all he knew.

"I am too much of an unbothered goddess to really care,
but I suppose you can send me something embarrassing that
I can laugh at with my friends (note: laugh at you, not with
you)," I typed back mechanically. I did it to proverbially
put a pacifier in his mouth. I knew he needed something, a
shred of attention, and sometimes when boys I liked left me
breadcrumbs of attention to eat up, it bought me a couple
hours, maybe days, of hope and satiety.

"I could get on my knees with women's underwear on
and you watch the scene," he offered. "Or I can do something
I've never done for You. For example, last year, a Domme
wanted me to lick a public toilet seat and then hit my balls

with a wooden spoon. But I didn't have the nerve. I would do that for You. No matter how painful or humiliating."

None of this was my jam at all. I could watch open-heart surgery without vomiting into a bucket, but a man hitting his own balls at my expense? Not for me. I had never known of someone wanting my attention that badly, so anyone who chased it, to me, was delusional. Like, bro: all I have to offer is a couple crumbly Nature Valley granola bars at the bottom of my purse.

I heard from him a couple days after that exchange, and he apologized profusely for being depressed. My first inclination was to feel sympathy and pity for him, but his ability to name his emotion, his overall state of being, was the first step in organizing it into something more manageable, tangible. I hope his ability to safely explore his identity with me eliminated some of his shame, which we all know festers in the dark. We're all just looking to be accepted, whether we're face down-ass up on a volleyball court to get our crushes to notice us, whether we're admiring porn stars not for the shape and dimensions of their labia but for their confidence to reveal the totality of themselves in a way we've been taught to be ashamed of, or whether we were raised in an unusual family structure that has us seeking out similar power dynamics because it's all we know. Unlike Travis, I might not need noise-canceling headphones to drown out the sound of sex in my house. But trust me, I could use the noise-canceling headphones to drown out the lies my brain tells me about myself that I'll never be good enough, not even for a man who's willing to hit his balls for me with a wooden spoon.

Chapter 5

SELLING MYSELF SHORT

In fifth grade, *Lererin* Zisman asked the students to pair up with a partner of the opposite sex for a Yiddish folk song dance lesson. I looked to my right where my blue-eyed crush Alex sat, his tiny legs folded neatly like a Buddhist statue in his plastic orange chair.

"Don't even think about it. You're way too tall," he said.

I was so petrified that blood left my brain and went straight to my cheeks. He turned away and continued to pry staples out of a long-division handout with surgical precision. While everyone else occupied themselves pairing up like animals boarding Noah's ark, I ran to the bathroom so no one could see what Alex saw. What I saw.

When I pushed open the last stall, the intention was to just sit with my head in my hands, but some sort of Pavlovian effect triggered my bladder when I saw the toilet anyway. I lowered my gym shorts under my tunic and spent the next several minutes peering at the painted-over graffiti on the walls, which, predictably, featured a collection of two first initials bound by plus signs, enveloped in fat, faded hearts. I doodled the letter A so frequently in the margins of my notebook, a public display would undermine the sanctity of it all, and maybe even jinx my already limited chances.

My breathing softened within the confines of the stall. Bathroom breaks were hard to come by in *Lererin* Zisman's class, who made us hold it in until the bell. This was my idea of seven minutes in heaven because it didn't require my crush to develop whiplash just to look up at me.

It wasn't until I spotted a dark shadow that I lowered my eyes from the wall downward.

"That's not good," I stated out loud, suddenly feeling very caged into the stall walls.

I instinctively balled up a fistful of single-ply toilet paper and placed it on the crotch of my underwear, hoping each additional layer would offset its chalkboard-like texture and bring me some comfort. If I couldn't see the mess, it would go away, I thought. The visual didn't quite match anything I had seen in those cartoonish anatomy textbooks well-meaning parents buy their kids at the first sprout of pubic hair. As far as I knew, the marks on my underwear were a product of not wiping properly during recess, because a) kids are not known for their pristine anal hygiene and b) I tended to throw '90s-style tantrums if I missed a single minute of sexually charged tag in the schoolyard, so bathroom breaks—besides this one, of course—were short and to the point.

I flushed, washed my hands, and returned to my classroom, which was now empty. Had I been sitting there that long? Outside, I spotted my classmates selecting teams for our daily game of sexually charged tag. From my vantage point, Alex looked even smaller than he usually did, gesticulating wildly as he bolted after a bite-sized girl from our class. For the second time in an hour, my body came in between me and what I loved.

The following day would have been your ordinary brand of elementary school hell if it weren't for that stubborn gravy-like stain rearing its ugly head yet again. I had since showered thoroughly, so it couldn't have been yesterday's stain, I reasoned. I coped with my bodily confusion the only way tweens know how: I wrote in my purple feathered diary. There was no way I could articulate what I saw out loud without being overcome by a feeling of guilt and shame.

I wrote that it looked like someone put a sword to my vagina in an attempt to merge the aesthetics of Georgia O'Keefe and Jackson Pollock onto one Fruit of the Loom canvas. I hypothesized that had someone actually violated me in my sleep, I probably deserved it, because if

Alex thinks I'm a tall ogre who isn't even worthy as a
Yiddish folk dance partner, I couldn't be worth much at
all. Similar to when ostriches dip their heads into a hole
in the ground and think no one can see them, if I just
buried the stain in toilet paper, I could pretend it never
happened.

My final sentiment surprised me, even as I wrote it:
"What happened to me was as if my vagina yelled too
loudly and hurt itself," read the squiggly handwriting in
light purple pen that matched the feathers perfectly. There
was something inherently magical and awe-inspiring
about an autonomic function leaving tangible traces of
its work. We breathe, we blink, but those impulses are
all fleeting whispers. My blood was a political statement
my brain had no idea it wanted to make. My body was
on its own trajectory, impervious to what Alex wanted.
But of course, you couldn't tell any of that to my ten-
year-old self without her suggesting you talk to the hand,
girlfriend.

I might have been ten, but I wasn't clueless. I knew
enough about the reproductive system to know shit stains
don't travel up your labia unless you've been grinding on
the arm of your couch to "Dirrty" by Christina Aguilera.
Up until then, the only blood I knew was that of Band-Aids
over chafed knees that most definitely resulted from a particularly aggressive match of sexually charged tag. No one
except for Sabrina with the Big Boobs had gotten her period
yet. This was an orifice I shouldn't have had to think about
until my first Women's March, earliest.

When I called Jenna and Diana to complain about my newfound fertility (of course at age ten, I used the words "blood everywhere am I dying help??") my yappy little playmates were, as I predicted, at a loss for advice that wouldn't humiliate me into an early death.

"I don't know what to say other than that I think you can get one of those diaper things from the nurse," said Jenna through the translucent blue landline she kept by her bed.

I imagined having to carry stacks of pads down the hall, clinging them tightly to my chest like schoolbooks.

"There's got to be a better way," I said.

Next lunch, I skipped tag to conduct research. I tiptoed to the back of the library, which housed the anatomy textbook I resorted to when I needed to psychologically rub one out. It featured a diagram of a man's buttocks, scrotum, and meatus (a term I proudly relayed to my friends). Beside it, a mock-up of a vagina, vulva ("Wait, Mom, like the car?"), and two sets of labia glared up at me. I flipped a few pages further into the book, quietly anticipating the information I was hoping for.

MENSTRUATION
Highlights you should know!
- Your uterus lining sheds and releases one egg each month.
- Cramps can be painful, but acetaminophen and a heating pad can help.
- Wash your hands before inserting a tampon so as not to introduce any bacteria into your vagina.

- Girls tend to experience a growth spurt right before their period, and shortly thereafter stop growing.
- You are now a woman.

Woman, woman, woman.

I pocketed the book in my schoolbag without checking it out with the librarian. I was so tall I floated out of there. No one could tag me if they tried.

Unsurprisingly, that self-administered sex ed lesson didn't have much of a lasting impact on my body image, but something else did change within me. Every time I felt the urge to saw off my developing curves or retreat into infancy for one week a month, I let that word *woman* echo in my mind as a reminder that it's okay to change, it's okay to grow. (Luckily, growing into a woman simultaneously meant that I stopped growing, my height culminating to a peak just when I needed it to slow down most). But spending my formative years looking like the weird one made it nearly impossible to shed that identity even when boys would compliment my looks.

Even though I no longer heard the words "tall" or "fat" hurled at me, I spent the next six years waiting for my many crushes to sign on to MSN Messenger after school when talking to them in class elicited existential dread. Interacting with them behind the screen was a way to make them hopefully forget what I looked like—whether they thought I was pretty or weird or both—and fall in love with me instead. For the longest time, my display picture was a box of Tampax, just so there were no surprises as to what potential suitors would be getting themselves into should they wish to proceed with me offline.

I had reconnected with Alex at a party in high school. We were the only ones to abstain from smoking weed. It's not that I was a goody-goody. Far from it, actually. I just didn't want anything to interfere with our perfect conversation free of any awkward silences about who had nicer blue eyes and why Protest the Hero was the best way to dip your toes into death metal if you come from a jazz background. He wasn't smoking because last time he hit a bong, he "greened out," leaving trails of puke across his friend's walkway. Confident in our connection, I suspected that excuse came secondary to wanting to make a great impression on me.

The night ended too early (curfews are the OG cock-blocks), so we continued our coy banter the only way I knew how. We spent hours upon hours a day online dissecting the intricacies of our family dynamics, our siblings, and our plans after high school. He was the only crush to ever indulge me in a seven-hour MSN Messenger conversation, so naturally I bound our first initials by plus signs, enveloped in fat, faded hearts that would one day get painted over on a bathroom stall.

Unable to suppress my longing for this person, I eschewed my sad habit of leading the entirety of my relationships online and asked him to hang out in person. I spent four hours choosing an outfit, settling on black leggings and a dark purple T-shirt with floral cutouts. My parents wouldn't be home, but I omitted that information. I wanted it to seem like a totally not-big-deal that I, a teenage girl, routinely asked guy friends to come over to shoot the shit and play video games. Plus, I didn't want to put any pressure on him to act a certain way. He didn't need to know I wanted him like *that*.

He showed up on his bike sweating profusely, even though the ride couldn't have been longer than eight minutes. We exchanged pleasantries, but I didn't say much. I couldn't. I was positively frozen in time without my backspace key as a crutch. So we did what all kids do. We sat in front of the TV, settling on a random show that neither of us have ever watched nor heard of, and pretended to look enthralled.

Feeling invincible in the dark, save for the glow of my parent's VHS player, I placed a hand on his knee. I turned to look at him. His eyes were already on me, hungrily. I knew he wasn't going to give me anything else besides a look from those intoxicating, warm blue eyes, so I took matters into my own hands. I wrapped my arms around his broad shoulders and kissed him lightly, but that slow, easy pace didn't last long. He reciprocated by open-mouth kissing me with such fervor I had no choice but to deep-throat his tongue if I wanted any oxygen to reach my lungs.

I pushed into his athletic chest so as to come up for air and shot back with one of those knowing glances he couldn't stop raving about over MSN. Up to my childhood bedroom we went, my stuffed animals littering the top of my twin bed like rose petals.

I had never been fully naked with anyone before, and felt hot with shame akin to the type that flooded me when I couldn't even get him to consider me as a Yiddish folklore dance partner. Even though he exceeded me in height by a full foot now, my spine ached from reflexively curling into myself in his presence. My internal organs felt bruised from sucking in. *Woman, woman, woman.*

"My god, you're such a woman," he said, biting his lower lip and looking me up and down. I didn't know how, or if, I should reciprocate any comments about his body. Cool scrotum? Nice meatus? With his eyes glued to me, I mimicked a burlesque dancer, ironically swiveling my hips every which way. Before I could continue my amateur show, he pinned me down and continued to kiss me with such enthusiasm I began to think he was high on something for wanting me so badly. Delusional for worshipping me.

The kissing veered on athletic, and a well-timed cough could no longer mask my hunger pangs.

"Excuse me, one sec. Just going to go to the bathroom super quick," I said.

I ran down to the kitchen, wearing nothing but my Bat Mitzvah ring, and shoved an entire banana into my mouth in one bite. Then came the mouthwash. He couldn't know I do something as disgusting as *eat*. Ah, much better.

"Where were we?" he asked, leading me back to my comically teddy-lined bed.

"Right here," I said, running my fingers across his pillowy lower lip.

Our naked bodies never actually touched while we kissed, like repelling magnets of similar polarity. I could have changed that, but I was done doing the initiating for the night. I couldn't risk having him feel my fleshy hips or thighs before swiftly putting his Aeropostale shirt back on and leaving. I lived for these liminal spaces that required no defining. But I would have felt a lot more euphoric had the banana fully quelled my hunger. And I wasn't going to let a moment like this pass me by because I decided to starve myself today.

"Oh shoot, forgot something downstairs. Hold on," I said. He didn't even look confused, which was confusing. I rummaged through the kitchen cabinets and found a rusty can opener. I flung open a can of tomato soup and sucked it down like cold juice on a dry airplane. Anything to coat my stomach so I can actually be a human being for this person. *Woman, woman, woman.*

Finally energized, I had the mental clarity to see him in a whole new light when I reentered my room. Like a post-nut clarity minus the nutting. His cheekbones glistened under my lobster-shaped lamp. His hands, contrary to his thin build, were strong and sturdy. They grabbed me, but I pulled away. We had to get going.

"My parents will be home any minute," I said. Not wanting to cut the night any shorter than it needed to be, I asked him to join me for a walk in the moon-lit park by my house. We reminisced about our reunion as the only two sober people at a party, noting how unusual it was to skip out on substances that were so hard to come by at that age.

"Why get drunk when your eyes are so intoxicating?" he said. I slapped him playfully. He pissed on a tree.

* * *

The following week, I hadn't gotten any texts. I bolted to my bedroom every day after school to catch him on MSN, hoping primitive technology was to blame for his radio silence. But I knew in my banana-and-tomato-soup-lined gut something else was happening here.

Ghosting wasn't yet a term in 2007 that I could use to characterize the experience and thus use as a starting place to heal. It's in part why I was proud of Travis years later for being able to name his depression. Naming is the first step. I just didn't know that was a thing. I knew about not giving away the cow, and whatever else Mother Goose dreamed up to shame women out of seeking pleasure. But how could my perfect night devolve into nothing after not having given away so much as a kiss, a glance, a conversation, let alone milk from a proverbial cow? I gave him nothing, so how could he have gotten what he wanted? Girls who kissed boys and engaged them in hours of thought-provoking conversation didn't wait by silent phones. They were asked out on second dates. They were texted back. Acknowledged.

I couldn't move on from the rejection without a reason, so I latched onto the only thing that has ever, without fail, gotten in between me and what I love: my body. My legs as they jiggled mercilessly under the light of my harsh lobster-shaped lamp. My stomach as it protruded after a banana and sip of soup. My double chin as I laughed, and laughed, and laughed some more at his jokes, which would have not been funny at all had I actually gotten off. An actual post-nut clarity.

So much time had lapsed since he messaged me again that MSN was defunct, and Facebook Messenger was the platform of choice.

"I've wanted to talk to you for a while now, but I didn't know how," he began, not bothering with the formalities with which he dazzled me at my doorstep seven years before.

"What do you mean, 'Didn't know how?' You open a chat bubble and type," I said.

Normally I would have waved it off and excused him for his silence. But unwarranted politeness never got me anywhere, and it certainly wouldn't now.

"I had so much fun that night, and all those hours staying up late talking, that I didn't know how to proceed. I thought you might have wanted us to turn into something more, and I wanted that too. But instead I choked."

"I appreciate you acknowledging what you did because not many people would," I said. "But it was a really, really shitty thing to do."

"You deserve the truth," he said.

This is where I anticipated a laundry list of copout excuses like "I needed to find myself," "I had just gotten out of a relationship," "I needed to try ayahuasca in the Peruvian jungle," "I needed to be alone."

But it was none of those things.

In true "us" fashion, we spoke for several more hours reminiscing about that one night with the contactless nudity when we panted and laughed as we bolted out of my parents' home, what we had been up to the past few years, what bands we were listening to, who we were and who we wanted to be, before he got more honest with me than he had with anyone in his entire life.

"Why are you telling me this?" I said. "Why now?"

"You were the only one to ever listen to me," he said, "and I was scared to ask you to listen to me when I needed you most."

It all started when he was four years old. His sister, who was eleven years older, would babysit him every week. He remembered how she would call each of his five siblings down into her room in the basement, one at a time. He assumed she asked his younger sister to play with dolls, or come up with Spice Girls dances. But his visits were far different from a standard sibling hangout filled with shared hobbies. He didn't know that it was abnormal that she would direct him to go higher or lower all over her body during massages she asked him to perform. After all, "As someone who looked up to her, I was just excited that she wanted to spend time with me at least," he told me during that long-overdue Facebook chat. But he knew something was off when she would unbutton her bra and demand he place his hands on her breasts. "If I hesitated or didn't obey, she'd get mad and tell me things like she'll tell my parents I was misbehaving and I'd get in trouble," he said.

My stomach was in my throat as he confided in me. I wanted to reach for him and tell him he's not broken and it's not his fault. I stayed silent and continued to listen for a long time, the way I could have listened years before if only he would have let me.

"I remember her telling me to put my hands lower until eventually they were inside her sweats and touching her inside her underwear," he continued. "And then on one of the last instances, she made me lie down naked on the cold bathroom floor and she put me inside her and started to yell at me to move faster. Terrified, I remember the edge of the entrance tiles digging into me."

"So how did you escape?" I asked, on the off chance that recounting this nightmare would provide some form of closure.

"I mustered the courage to say I had to pee," he said. "She tried to make me go while she just stayed in the bathroom with me. And when I couldn't go, I got yelled at and brought to tears."

He doesn't remember how long the abuse went on for, or how many times it happened. What he does remember is the way any wrong move warranted discipline. And it was a feeling so overwhelmingly painful, he said he couldn't risk making a wrong move around me, too.

All this time I had the audacity to blame his silence on my body—be it my height in Yiddish class, my blood in the schoolyard, and my body in my bed. My body followed me around wherever I went, so naturally it was an easy scapegoat I could use to find meaning in misfortune. Plus, turning the blame inward was my way of experiencing the full spectrum of pain and sadness I've always been predisposed to chase without tarnishing any relationships in the process. Because God forbid I turned off the polite performance and ruffled any feathers.

My body wasn't the problem. It never was. It was my inability to extend that level of attention outward to someone else. The boy who called me too tall when all I wanted was a Yiddish dance partner wasn't admonishing my body; he was rebuilding the wall of armor around himself that his sister eroded when she, that very week, slapped his naked, raw body on the bathroom floor when he didn't perform to her liking.

In hating my body all these years, I've ascribed to it an importance it does not merit. I'd have rather used my moments slouching in front of Alex in fifth grade to stand tall, present to him my most authentic self, and send the message that we can dive into the deepest corners of his heart together, and come back out stronger for it. I'd have rather used my first moments as a woman advocating for my reproductive health at the nurse's office instead of locking myself in a bathroom stall, hanging my head in shame, and stealing anatomy books from the library to read behind closed doors. I'd have rather used those euphoric moments kissing Alex in my childhood bedroom to merge our bodies together. Like magnets of opposing polarity, neither of us were broken if we could be broken together.

Chapter 6

SOMETHING'S WEIGHING ON ME

"I can't eat past seven in the evening. I'll gain weight."

"I'm so fucking fat today."

"Bagels are fattening. Are bananas?"

"Sugar is the devil. Fat used to be, but it depends what kind."

"I gained a pound last week so order without me."

"Stop making me eat bread."

"I tore my ankle on the treadmill and now I don't know how to get my cardio."

I wish these were sound bites from brunch with my friends. Alas, they were mantras my father said on loop in our home growing up. He theorized that unless he restricted entire food groups and fixated on calories, he'd gain back all ninety pounds he had lost in his thirties when his blood pressure results worried his physician.

When most people picture their dads, they see a pair of sturdy legs dotted in camel-colored steel-toe boots peeking out from beneath a car as he tinkers with its tires, or maybe a loosened collar and tie slung around broad shoulders. Sure, my dad has embodied those heteronormative tropes on several occasions. But when I think of him, which is every time I need reassurance that, yes, I am allowed to eat these cookies as long as I work out afterward, I see puppy dog eyes rife with worry and guilt, his concave cheeks chomping down on roasted unsalted almonds.

"Calories don't count if you're standing up," he said with one hand funneling tasteless nutrients into his mouth, the other gripping onto a love handle like he was wringing out a dish towel. I knew he was joking, but as the man who is competent enough to remember how much in taxes I owe down to the decimal, and who has a track record of only making stellar life decisions (like, hello, his wife is a snack), I accepted everything he said as gospel.

Growing up, I saw my dad's relationship with food as completely normal, and nothing noteworthy enough to define him. To me, he was always the baseball fanatic, the accountant, the comedian, everyone's friend. But if my dad could routinely ball handfuls of loose flesh into his fists, complain about what he felt and saw, and still lead a seemingly normal—if not admirable—life, surely self-deprecation was my ticket to being just like him.

I was three years old when I noticed my thighs touch for the first time. I didn't have the language to complain out loud like my dad did, but his mind-set made so much sense to me that I adopted it as my own. I couldn't be the baseball-slinging son he'd always wanted, but I could be something else he never knew he wished for. I could be his confidante, his shoulder to lean on, his equal teammate in this violent sport we call restriction-fueled weight loss.

During one of my last weekends living at home as a young adult, he caught me fawning over the latest *Vogue* September issue. My shirt had been lifted just above my diaphragm where I was tracing each rib like piano keys. The more of them I felt, the louder the music. He knew exactly what I was doing, because it's something he does himself.

"You know, even good-looking people you admire like Scarlett Johansson and Brad Pitt take very offensive shits," he said without an ounce of sarcasm. "And plus, they don't even look like themselves in real life, what with the retouching, and the this, and the that." When dads talk about technology, they make about as much sense as a Google translation—you get the gist of what they're saying, but the syntax is cringe-worthy.

Despite the gibberish, I heard him loud and clear: the people we worship are flawed, too. My dad and his "perfect" healthy diet. Celebrities and their purchased symmetry. We see only the fragments of their bodies and their lives proven to be most profitable. Somewhere under those designer clothes are butts that expel ungodly things no matter how Pilates-taut they look. The celebrities in magazines I worship dream of looking like the Photoshopped versions of themselves in real life, too. But how could I possibly listen to my dad wax poetic about bodily confidence when he demonstrated so little of a grasp on it himself? What did it mean to worship someone who only showed you the fragment of themselves they thought was most marketable, be it a stranger on a perfectly choreographed Instagram feed or a parent?

* * *

I never felt like a "real" eating disorder patient, so I never bothered seeking help. I wasn't emaciated, nor did I ever develop lanugo, a thin layer of peach fuzz coating my skin. At many points in my life, I've been able to order pasta at a restaurant without having a complete meltdown, so surely, nothing could have been wrong enough with me to warrant medical help. Sure, the DSM-V now recognizes atypical anorexia as a condition wherein the patient meets all criteria for anorexia nervosa yet possesses a body weight that's either within or above range. But if it wasn't a term broadcasted on #thinspo pro-anorexia pages, I didn't want to hear from it. The only images of eating disorders I'd ever seen as of age fourteen, when my food phobias peaked, were paparazzi shots of Mary-Kate Olsen gazing doe-eyed over a bone-thin shoulder paired with tabloid copy that detailed her admittance into a rehab facility. No one looked at me and got worried enough to send me away to Arizona.

Illnesses are supposed to make you feel like perpetual shit. It made no sense to me that the eating disorder voice in my head could make me feel so good when I obeyed it. I was high on my own mind all the time. The lighter I got, the less physical and emotional effort I expended to comfortably exist in public. In ninth grade, I let my boyfriend see me naked for the first time. And sure, I was embarrassed about the amount of pubic hair I hadn't yet ever shaved, but I could proudly flaunt my newfound thigh gap beneath. I posted seductive pictures of myself on MySpace, very much disturbed by the attention I received from strange men, but reveling in it in a sick way, nonetheless. I made internet friends on secret Xanga blogs, sharing our tips for surviving on an apple a day, a cucumber, too, if we felt like spoiling ourselves. We posted daily challenges (Only eat with your left hand today, that way you won't want to do it!!!). We right-clicked and saved images of bony girls and stowed them away in secret folders labeled things like "Hebrew homework." On these message boards, I wasn't the Weird One. I wasn't the Perv. I was flowergirl123, who consistently, without fail, met her published goal weight for the week. Behind my keyboard, I was invincible. None of the other numbered and underscored screen names could see how much of a fraud I was.

To distract my internet friends from the fact that I wasn't posting images of my body, which to me looked far larger than theirs, I shared my poetry. I blushed as the likes and comments flooded in. I was finally a member of their community the same way sergeants welcome new soldiers into the army. I shared material they could right-click and save. Thinspiration, us insiders called it.

We Are Going to Be Very Thin Today
By Marissa Miller

We are going to be very thin today. We are not going to go over four hundred and fifty calories. We are going to snap rubber bands against our wrists. We are going to tame the human within through punishment and torment. We are going to cut up magazines and ignore everything they say about full breasts and childbearing hips. We are going to lie down and hallucinate, high off hunger, and implode until we are one of the molecules that once composed us, our bones clanking dishes inside of us, we are carcasses covered in skin. Emphatic youth. And we are beautiful. Cold and blue. Ocean eyes. We are not going to leave footprints in the snow. We are going to force ourselves to laugh at pathetic YouTube videos in order to engage our abdominals. We are going to cry the sodium away, away, away and instead of drowning we will float, because that's what winners do. We are going to be warriors and we will never sleep, no, not until we are victorious against the supermarkets that are trying to kill us all with kindness. With preservatives, with nitrates, sulfates, and sad chickens that once spent a full 72 hours in each other's excrement. We will chew when people are watching, and spit when they are not. We are going to brush our fangs. We are going to be beautiful. We are going to be very thin today if it's the last thing we do.

"Honey, you have an eating disorder," one of my oldest friends Clara said one day after brunch, over a decade after I got locked out of my flower123 account on Xanga and couldn't be bothered to reset the password. But certainly not forgotten were the pages upon pages of photos in my Hebrew homework folder of what my limbs were supposed to look like, lenses zoomed in on fragments of people, just the correct parts, and specific diagrams detailing how to get there even if it killed you. I had cried in Clara's Honda Civic after we paid our bill. I couldn't believe I let myself have cheese in my omelet. I was supposed to ask for extra spinach instead, and like my password and my plight to be the right weight and right size, I forgot. Idiot, idiot, idiot. *Woman, woman, woman.*

Clara's entire aesthetic is summarized by leopard print and Betty Boop. She has so many remarkable qualities that her internship working for the future prime minister of Canada is not even close to the most impressive thing she's ever done.

"You can't just diagnose me, Clara. You think you know everything," I said defiantly. I knew she was right, but admitting it meant I had to—or should—be proactive about overcoming it. If eating disorders truly were illnesses, I couldn't just leave mine to fester like a black mold crawling out of a crisp white windowpane.

"I've known you had one since you slept over in second grade and we ordered McDonald's Quarter Pounders with cheese, and you had to call your mom to ask for permission to eat it. I don't know what she said, but you ended up just watching me eat mine, and I've never seen you eat a hamburger since," she said. "We will get through this together."

It wasn't long before I found myself calling every specialist in the city. For most treatment clinics, waitlists were as long as a year. Turns out I really wasn't the only one. But I couldn't wait that long to finally seek treatment, because like ordering a cheesy omelet without giving it much thought, I didn't want to give myself a chance to talk myself out of treatment. I wanted to know the joy Clara feels when she bites into greasy fast food. But it's not even joy I seek. I want that everydayness. Nothingness. Like brushing teeth. Unpacking groceries. Folding laundry. The message boards I frequented had long shut down. The only voices encouraging me to self-destruct were no longer sick strangers on the internet. They were my own.

A cordial, raspy voice answered the phone when I called a clinic located in Westmount, the ritzy part of town where kids' allowances exceed that of my freelance salary. I felt okay traversing to that side of town because it's already where I went up to the fifth floor with all the other "crazies" three years earlier to see my therapist Francesca. The intake worker asked me dozens of specific questions that I felt bizarre sharing over the phone. It felt both more intimate and far less removed than posting to anonymous strangers on the internet. Instead of just my typeface on a social media platform, she could hear my actual voice utter the words, "I'm addicted to laxatives because I don't know how to make myself throw up but I would totally throw up if I could, so don't judge me. I've started shitting blood but that won't make me stop. I'm also incapable of eating a single piece of food without completely hating myself, and if I go a day without working out, I start thinking about how my day was completely wasted and I shouldn't have even bothered waking up in the morning." Shocked that I didn't even have to lie about the severity of my situation just for them to take me seriously, it wasn't even a week until I got my first appointment at the eating disorder clinic.

"I need something more," I told Marjorie during our seventh session together. She was kind enough to take me on in a city swarming with people who never make it to the top of the waiting list until it's too late. Her voice was so gentle I often couldn't hear it, but maybe that was my scared, beating heart ringing out the sound in my ears. Sure, my weekly weigh-ins and food journals helped track my progress, but I seemed to continue to disappoint her week after week. "Marissa, you've got to try harder to stop purging," Marjorie said. "We need you to stop."

"I know I've definitely met someone with an eating disorder," I told her, "but no one's ever been open about it with me. The only reference point I have is Mary-Kate Olsen circa 2004, and if you put us side by side, we look like we're struggling with two separate illnesses. I need to see myself in someone."

The sound of my beating heart continued to thump in my ears as I climbed the steps of a shiny gray building on Monkland Avenue, Notre-Dame-de-Grâce's most gentrified main vessel. The neighborhood still managed to retain certain bones bearing old-world charm, making the group therapy appointment Marjorie suggested feel a lot less threatening. It was a street I frequented almost every day, so while the Febreeze-scented building felt familiar, I was about to come face-to-face with yet another set of strangers. Strangers I couldn't hide from behind a keyboard and a screen name. Strangers who would see in plain sight that I'm a fraud and that I don't have a real eating disorder because I don't look like Mary-Kate Olsen circa 2004.

"Welcome to the group," said Hadassah with a sweet, closed-mouth smile. She was far less distant than previous therapists I had. I almost wanted to ask her how her weekend was, or what she did with her family, or what her plans were for the Jewish holidays. Unlike Hadassah, Marjorie would never entertain that kind of line of questioning. As part of my outpatient "team," the plan was for both Marjorie and Hadassah to share information about my progress—or lack thereof. So I abstained from getting too friendly because I didn't want to give Hadassah any reason to tell Marjorie that I'm a lonely freak who tries too hard to befriend therapists.

It was nearly impossible to abstain from comparing myself to the other women in the group. I couldn't stop thinking, not about where I was in my own progress, but how I stacked up to them. On the one hand, I wanted to be the one closest to recovery because I'd be that much closer to feeling what it's like to eat a sandwich without politiciz-ing it. On the other, I wanted to be the sickest one in the room to prove I had a right to be there.

"You have to wish me luck, guys," I said to my eating disorder group one evening in early December 2019. I was days away from my yearly trip with my family. This time it would be a week at an all-inclusive resort in Mexico, my ninety-one-year-old bubby included. My mom wanted to include her in our plans in the off—but very real—chance this would be our last opportunity for us to be the five of us together in one place, like time had stopped in 1994 when my best friend of a baby sister was born and we had a whole lifetime's worth of memories to make. One of these memories just happened to be a trip to a popular spring break destination. I love an open bar as much as the next guy, but if it meant gaining weight, I would have rather stayed home with my cats.

"What's your game plan?" my dad nudged me as we lugged our tired bodies into the Italian buffet an hour after landing in Cancún. A nice Russian family lit the Chanukah candles at a table behind us, so I felt at home already. The familiarity of it all made the food seem less scary than if they were to have not been there.

"I'll probably just have the salad bar so that way I'm too full to order off the menu," I said. I knew exactly what he meant by "game plan."

As a food and nutrition writer for *Women's Health* (oh, the irony), I know the brighter the produce, the more antioxidants it tends to contain. But I also know that my dad lost twenty pounds this year by eating a diet of mainly fruits, vegetables, ancient grains and plant-based proteins, and weight loss is far more immediate, tangible, and sexy of a benefit I can enjoy than, say, reducing my risk of cardiovascular disease and inflammation. I piled my plate with so many vivid colors you wouldn't even need to drop acid to trip out looking at the bounty. My eyes shifted back and forth toward my dad's plate to see if our meals looked similar. If they did, surely I was doing something right.

I chewed on my salad, telling myself lies like, *It'll help prevent traveler's constipation! It'll boost my energy so I feel like making it to morning Aqua Fitness!* But none of those things happened. Instead, I went for seconds, grabbed a calzone from the buffet (I use the term "salad bar" loosely here), and shoveled it into my mouth before I could talk myself out of it. It was gone in two bites.

"We're here to support you," my mom said, placing a hand on mine at the table. She could sense the distress in my puppy dog eyes, the worry and guilt. "All from a slice of calzone?" she half said, half asked. But to me it was so much more than a calzone. The calzone represented my weakness, my inability to do the right thing like my well-to-do accountant father who lights up a room like the *shamash* on a Chanukiah.

"Tell us how you want us to support you," she continued after my strained silence. The "us" was the Royal We, which included my sister Michelle, my bubby, and oddly, my father. I told her I couldn't tell her how I wanted them to support me: that would be like asking someone to throw you a surprise party complete with your preferred color theme and playlist instead of having them figure out what you like themselves. I wanted the support to feel genuine and authentic, as raw as her maternal instinct would allow. There had to be a sort of clinical response to her question. Half-committed to my treatment, the only support I really wanted was the kind that would tell me the calzone wasn't so bad after all because I did three hours of spinning the day before. It didn't matter what the support looked like. Maybe just knowing support was available to me was enough.

The following morning I awoke not to bubby's snoring like I thought I would but to a nudge on the shoulder.

"We're going downstairs," my mom said. "Get dressed."

"But mom, my rule is that I can't eat until I've been awake for six hours and feel like I might pass out from hunger. I can't just eat on command."

"Sure you can," she smiled warmly.

I reluctantly slid into a cheap sundress and cardigan and took the elevator down to the buffet. It was basically the Litchfield Correctional Institution cafeteria from *Orange Is the New Black* had it been decorated in pineapples and sombreros. I sat alone at the sad beige table while my mom, Michelle, and bubby topped their plates with normal breakfast foods you'd see on a diner menu, and my dad loaded up a heaping plate of raw fruit.

"We thought you'd like this," Michelle said softly, offering me a plate of food as she returned to the table. The plate had a slice of whole wheat toast, avocado, some nuts, papaya, and a poached egg. The last time I was that touched, my best friend asked me to be a bridesmaid in her wedding.

I stared at the plate as if it were a Petri dish filled with bacteria under a lens. If I ate it, I'd just hate myself for the rest of the day and do unspeakable, self-mutilative things to get rid of the hate, I reasoned. But miraculously—or maybe predictably, because therapy is scientifically proven to work and isn't some made-up witchcraft—Hadassah's encouraging voice sounded louder in my ears than the eating disorder's: "You're always going to feel anxiety the deepest when you first take a risk, but the anxiety wanes the more and more you expose yourself to the fear, so you have to dive into it every day. And if you wait too long to take that risk again, your anxiety will revert back to square one. Don't lose that momentum."

If I don't jump into this Petri dish of anxiety headfirst, I thought, *a) I won't make it to Aqua Fitness, and b) I'll never get better.*

"What's a matter with you? *Ess! Ess mein kind!* Don't be silly!" my bubby said as if it made absolutely no sense to her that someone could be within several feet of food and not eat it all in one swift action. It soothed me to know she thought about food that way. Even though she had to endure horrific events and destitution throughout the war to appreciate abundance, her gift to me was the idea that food isn't my enemy but my means of survival, the same way it was hers.

I took tiny bites at a time. I couldn't deny Michelle the joy of watching her complicated, frustrating older sister finally do a thing most people seem to do just fine. Each bite tasted more metallic than the last, a sign my brain didn't want me to enjoy the foods (*Women's Health*–approved foods!) I genuinely love. But my brain wasn't on my side.

My brain told me I shouldn't eat, and that I need to rid my body of everything I do eat immediately afterward. And somehow, my brain also told me that line of thinking isn't problematic at all. Clearly, I couldn't trust it. It was time to give in to the people around me who seemed to know best. To let them support me in a way that feels as organic to them as a Whole Foods avocado.

From my peripheral vision, I noticed the look of sheer joy plastered across my mom and Michelle's faces as I continued to polish off the avocado toast, their approving nods feeling less infantilizing and more encouraging by the second. My bubby stared idly at the wall as she chewed the ricotta pancakes soft enough for her dentures. My dad followed the script my mom laid out for him: "You're doing great, Riss!"

I was weirdly excited to get back home, to let my digestive tract just be, to enjoy my friends' company without rushing out midsentence to go work out in a lonely hotel room. Beyond being a lot more dangerous (with a mortality rate of 10 percent, eating disorders are the most fatal of any mental illness, according to the National Institute of Mental Health), my eating disorder was hardly different from celebrities' pathological need to Photoshop their bodies. They reveal only the fragments of themselves that have historically earned networks, publicists, and publishing houses the most money. I push my weight down like I'm trying to drown a floatation device with the sole goal of feeling worthy of love.

If I wasn't so busy performing calorie calculations, I could see that love is right in front of me. It's in the surprise plates of avocado toast, it's in the pep talks, it's in the nudges on my shoulder gently waking me up from a restful sleep. As much as I desperately want to cling to our secret language ("Dessert is for losers!" "Dressing on the side!"), I'm finding new ways to connect with my dad that aren't rooted in illness. Digging him out of his disorder is in no way a feat I'm qualified to professionally undertake, nor is it a role as his child that I should even attempt. But for the first time this year, I've replaced lines like "Don't make me eat bread" and "I'm so fucking fat today" with "Dad, what you eat does not define you" and "Your weight is not a measure of success." A toxic relationship doesn't need to stay that way just because it's familiar like the rituals of a disorder. The transition might be shaky and it might take a little bit of time. But never for a moment have I regretted guiding him toward a world where burgers with white buns exist, and that enjoying them once in a while (or, who knows, maybe all the time?) is part of living a whole, complete life that's far more colorful than any plate of antioxidant-rich salad bar produce can ever achieve.

Chapter 7
THE F-WORD

"Fat" was at one point the most fear-inducing word I knew. But it doesn't sting as badly as "freelance."

If you're sitting next to me at a bar and your opening line is, "So, what do you do?" because you're lame and can't pick up women, if I'm not interested, I'll say I'm a freelance journalist. If I am interested, I'll tell you I'm a journalist.

I can't attach the F-word to my title, my identity, without feeling a sense of inferiority. "Oh, if she's freelance, she must be from the reject pile. She must be unbearable in an office." (I mean, they wouldn't be wrong; I'd want to pick my split ends incessantly and sit in my desk chair in the fetal position because my legs don't touch the ground. No one needs to know I need a goddamn seat belt for everyday, leisurely sitting.)

I never planned on working as a full-time freelancer. No one dreams of going to bed at 3:00 a.m. every day and wearing the same pair of pajama pants for six days straight (I'm sure there are unicorns out there who wear bras and pants with waistbands in the confines of their own homes, and I salute them). No one dreams of always being home when the mailman rings the doorbell, always having an excuse at the ready as to why you look worse than the trash raccoons eating on your lawn ("Looks like I have a cold again! This weather, amiright??"). But freelancing from home is exactly where I landed when I was laid off from my job as a social media manager at a modeling agency. My title sounded fancy, but I felt remarkably useless. My "strategy" was to have none. At the time, I thought it was so au courant to wing it, the way the most authentic social media accounts felt in aesthetic. In truth, my unwillingness to formalize a strategy was a way to justify not having to learn anything new, and instead completely improvise like I did while uploading tired memes to my own Instagram account while on the bus to that very job. No one told me it takes an incredulous amount of art direction to make a photo look unposed, that laissez-faire "too-cool" captions all undergo six rounds of workshopping. I was afraid to work at being the best I could be because I thought of all the pressure and responsibility that comes with being great. I thought everyone looked naturally perfect from my vantage point. Competing and losing would be far more embarrassing than abstaining from the race altogether.

My French wasn't good enough, they said, but I'm pretty sure a lot of it had to do with routinely asking my boss if I could use the empty boardroom to conduct interviews with sources for magazine pieces I was writing that had nothing to do with the actual job he was paying me to do. I could have easily and discretely waltzed into an empty room and conducted my interviews on my lunch break, but I wanted him to know I was so much more than the incompetent Anglophone he hired to putz around on TweetDeck for fifteen dollars an hour. I was a *journalist*.

I needed a plan once I returned my corporate laptop and shook hands good-bye with my coworkers. I was twenty-two and still living in my parents' house, which was equal parts normal if you can't afford a place on your own (read: fifteen dollars an hour), and equal parts inconvenient when you want to have boys over.

I didn't move to Toronto entirely because I wanted my own door with my own lock, but it did have something to do with it. After applying, following up, and following up some more, a senior editor at a major women's magazine offered me a digital internship with less than two weeks' notice. There was no time (or money) to find a place of my own. I would be staying on the couch of a friend of a friend of a friend. There would be no hooking up. There would be no doors, let alone locks. Just a futon in the middle of the living room, my suitcase a landfill overflowing in front of me.

Gabe came from a well-known Irish family who owned lots of property in Montreal. But with money comes the need to uphold a certain reputation, and being gay where everyone has high expectations of you and your family "wouldn't attract the right type of attention," he told me our first night as roommates.

Gabe was away on business the first week I crashed in his apartment in a shady area of town in Danforth. The first few hours after my family dropped me off to help me set up were dead quiet. The silence was conducive to a good night's sleep. But sleep never came. I heard the gunshots outside only a few feet below my fourth-floor bedroom window. My heartbeat caught up with the shots firing in quick succession until they were thumping in tune with one another. I lay awake that entire night, eyes wide open, completely still, listening to my heart beat in my ear against the pillow like an oncoming train.

* * *

Roger's Publishing was like the Hearst or Condé Nast of Canada but involved in far fewer scandals (read: class-action labor lawsuits) than its American counterparts. There was a hoity-toitiness to it that made me overly anxious about what I wore. Let's just say I've had lunch with my editors at *Vogue*, *Teen Vogue*, *Cosmopolitan*, and *Women's Health* at both the Hearst Tower and One World Trade, and was pleased and relieved to find my editors whom I worshipped so deeply over email could get on board with some of my more risky dad joke material in person, and even take part. Nothing like that would ever fly at Roger's Publishing.

On my first day, I arrived two hours earlier than my supervisor. No one told me what time my shift started, so I played it safe and got there for 8:30 a.m. I sat at an empty cubicle flipping through back issues of the magazine so I could dazzle my superiors with trivia they already knew and assumed I wouldn't. I wanted so badly to fit in that I wore mismatched prints, because that's what magazine editors do, according to the magazines they wrote.

"Hey Marissa, we're going to have you go into the backend and just relabel every image to boost SEO. Cool?" said an editor with pin-straight hair in a chunky-knit gray sweater sometime after 10:30 a.m. Her pants were gray, too. Her eyes, partly obscured by severe straight bangs, were sad and sallow. Gray, too.

The task was so menial it wouldn't have been unheard of to fall asleep mid-assignment. But every fiber of my being was on fire with adrenaline to compensate for my sleepless night, the sound of bullets punctuating each strained inhale as my ear pressed against the pillow. By noon, the woman in the gray sweater was suspicious of me when I asked her for a more challenging assignment. I wanted a byline, a name on the masthead, proof I existed. I wanted to be more than a faceless keyboard behind a modeling agency's social media account. I'd been an anonymous internet person on eating disorder message boards all throughout high school, and look where that got me.

Just knowing where I was headed to work every morning transformed me into a stallion powerhouse of a woman. I was a human superfood. I strutted like I was perpetually in heels even though I wore salt-stained Ugg boots on my commute. My posture was so straight I looked like I was constantly looking over someone's shoulder. I took up more space. Maybe even too much, I thought, mentally snapping a rubber band against my brain to minimize the egomania.

It was hard to shake my social media manager tendencies of yore. I loaded up TweetDeck on my Rogers-issued desktop even before logging into the magazine's content management system where my daily SEO project awaited me. My Twitter timeline was riddled with fellow newbie journalists announcing their new staff positions everywhere from local newspapers to Pulitzer prize–winning magazines. Here I was, backtracking from an office job to an internship, like a kid who couldn't read being held back a year in elementary school and getting to high school later than all his friends.

"Can you swing by my office?" said an email from an editor. It was not my editor with the pin-straight hair and gray sweater and gray everything else, but rather someone I had never met.

I swiveled around in my chair and took a deep, labored inhale. To limit our amount of back-and-forth, I consulted the coordinates listed in her email signature and headed straight for her office.

The hallway was long and white, not unlike the snowy path I walked to get to that publisher's building every morning. Rita's office was blooming with makeup samples spilling out of every corner of her shelf. This was the beauty department, I guessed.

"See this?" she said, rotating her desktop toward me before I could even get comfortable on the plush blue velvet chair facing her desk.

"Uh, yes," I stammered, squinting my eyes closer to her screen.

Her burgundy almond-shaped nails pointed to my Twitter profile, an avatar of my smiling face emblazoned above. That very page was open on my desktop, too, a cold and clinical hallway away.

"This, right here, is an example of what not to do," Rita said.

She didn't have to scroll for long to find the evidence. They were only a couple tweets in: "I'm a slut for SEO" and then "Always an intern, never an employee," they read.

The sad part is that as I was writing those tweets, they felt like some of my best work. They felt so accurate. Like, want to know who I really am? Check my Twitter.

"I . . . I'm so sorry," I offered. "I'm just so enthusiastic about the work here that I would give my entire being to it. And I see myself working here long-term. It's just that as an intern, I—"

"I don't want an explanation. I want you to know we monitor everyone's social media accounts and you have to be representative of our brand. You are not Marissa. You are the magazine," she said. "Flip through our magazine. Get to know us. We are not what you just wrote."

No amount of memorized magazine trivia to impress my supervisors could undo what I had done.

The only way I could squash that sick feeling in my abdomen was to leave the office an hour after the last employee. When I left the building, the sky was a beautiful plush blue velvet perfect for a beauty editor's office. Gabe greeted me when I got home.

"Here, this is what we're doing tonight." It looked like a vibrator of some sort. But knowing he wasn't into me like that, it could only be one other thing.

* * *

"How do I use it?"

"Press down. Like this," he said, filling his lungs with the vaporizer and expertly exhaling a succession of smoke rings.

It was nothing like the smelly weed I smoked at home that took an entire village to roll. First you had to find a flat surface. Then you had to find papers and a filter. Then you had to roll the damn thing without your hands shaking, but your hands were always shaking because your parents were always walking in on you at the wrong time. And if you did manage to roll it, smoke it, and discard of the evidence, you smelled like a skunk that escaped from an incinerator. Going down, this weed tasted like a nutty arugula salad that paired perfectly with Pinot. It was fresh, almost minty, my gums tingling and on fire at the same time.

"There's no way this is weed," I said. Like I had a clue.

"I swear. My buddy got me this new vape and it's a total game-changer," Gabe said. "You can smoke inside and basically whenever and wherever you want. Tell you what. Since you're not paying rent, you supply the groceries and weed." It felt like prostitution of sorts, but it sounded fair. We took hits of the vape on the futon I'd be sleeping on that night until the slightest sound was the funniest thing in the world. The tweets came to me, but they stayed in my Notes folder. If Toronto couldn't know who I really was, no one could.

I didn't want to have to rely on Gabe to use his vape. After all, it would be pretty pathetic to be indebted to him any more than I already was. So I learned how to roll. Really well. I pre-rolled joints and carried them around with me like a pack of cigarettes on the off chance I needed to get high right then and there because I got a threatening email from an editor or something. I kept them stashed away in my purse the same way others are littered with loose pieces of gum and capless lipstick. But I had a rule. No getting high at work. Ever.

The following morning at my desk, I was exhausted. In an SEO daze, I thought about the night before when I got the brand of high that sent me down a four-hour PornHub spiral. Though I had the libido of a fourteen-year-old boy, I had no intention of watching any videos like fourteen-year-old boys do. All I wanted to know was if any story lines were worth repurposing into poems.

"Oh shit, didn't see you there," I said, slamming my laptop shut while someone's bleached asshole was spread colonoscopy style on my screen.

"That's really fucking gross, Marissa," Gabe said, walking by my futon on the way to the bathroom to brush his teeth. "If you're going to do that shit in my house, you'll have to get the fuck out before I actually kill you."

The word "kill" hung in the air like a bullet cutting through the windowpane a few feet below our fourth-floor apartment. Like my reaction to most traumatic incidences, I shut down my computer and my brain, and promptly fell asleep, but not before promising myself I'd deal with it tomorrow. Maybe.

I left for work earlier than usual that morning so I wouldn't have to perform the awkward dance of pretending nothing happened the night before as Gabe brewed coffee in the kitchen. I used the extra thirty quiet minutes in the office to browse for a new apartment on Craigslist. It didn't matter where. I could deal with outdoor gunshots. I could deal with stiff futons. What I couldn't deal with was a friend who wanted me dead.

I suddenly heard a knock on the back wall of my cubicle. I minimized my apartment search browser with the knee-jerk swiftness of a teenage boy watching porn. It was unusual for the pin-straight-haired editor to knock. She usually descended upon me like Santa Claus landing with a loud thump in the hot mouth of a fireplace.

"Hey, so here's the deal," she began in a whisper. "We're going to have you clean up that last batch of wellness evergreen pieces in the CMS, and then we'll send you on your merry way, mmmkay?"

"Oh, but that won't take me more than a couple hours, three hours tops. I'll be done before noon. Feel free to throw anything my way after that so I have enough work for the day," I said.

"I'm assuming you haven't heard," she said apologetically.

"Heard what?"

"So, basically, this morning, the Ontario government passed a legislation declaring unpaid internships illegal in the province, so we're obligated to terminate your internship effective immediately."

What the fresh hell was going on? Within a span of six hours, my life was threatened, and then the only thing that gave me a sense of purpose was taken away from me.

"But I want to stay," I said. "I don't care if you don't pay me. It doesn't bother me. I just want to have somewhere to show up every morning and be around this smart team of editors and continue to learn from you guys and try my hardest to be the best writer I could be. Please. Don't I have a say in this? This internship means everything to me."

My editor clasped her hands and offered a tight-lipped smile.

"That's all well and good, Marissa, but we're just not hiring right now. And you deserve to be paid. You're a good writer with a bright future ahead of you. You're one of the best interns we've ever had. Enthusiastic to a fault, even. I mean, look at you, begging for assignments. This just means more time for you to pursue paid opportunities," she said. I never thought she'd dangle a string of compassion toward me for the first time just as she was letting me go. I almost wished she told me to get the fuck out before she actually kills me. That way saying good-bye wouldn't be so hard.

"We can't pay you, but here's a token of our appreciation," she said. She sped-walk back to her desk and returned with a shopping bag the width of my desk. It overflowed with makeup samples, the ones that bloomed out of shelves above Rita's head as she pointed out what was wrong with my Twitter feed, what was wrong with me. It felt like I was inheriting a family heirloom. Essie, OPI, Revlon, Lancôme, Philosophie, Clinique, MAC, Maybelline, L'Oreal. The value must have exceeded whatever I spent on groceries and weed in the last three months. I almost felt unworthy of it. Guilty. Like my creative and journalistic contributions to their magazine didn't count unless I emotionally *and* financially suffered.

"Wow, this is incredible," I said, leafing through the primers, top coats, and lip glosses of varying consistencies. I don't think she deliberately gave me a parting gift to soften the blow, but it did eliminate much of the sting like a quick hit of Valium before a plane ride.

I boarded the empty subway two hours later, holding the pillar of makeup products between my legs as the train shook beneath my salt-stained Uggs. All alone at noon on a Tuesday, it was a luxury to cry so freely in public. My life up to that point had been a series of dismissals, never having the chance to move on from anything on my own terms. If only I could hold onto experiences as tightly as I did that bag of free makeup.

I wasn't expecting to see Gabe sitting at the kitchen table. He was sweating profusely, and I could see an inch of his crotch hanging out of his boxers.

"What are you doing here?" he asked. He was lighting a cigarette and exhaled it toward the closed window.

"I could ask you the same thing," I shot back.

"I haven't gone to work all week. I've been too depressed. What's your excuse?" he said.

"I'm really sorry to hear that. Do you want to talk about it? I just got laid off from my internship, so, looks like it's me and you in this depressive mess together," I said. I waited for him to pull up a chair in solidarity. That's how misery works. It thrives in multiples.

"There's nothing to talk about," he said. "I need you to get the fuck out before I do something really bad to you or to myself."

I couldn't tell which option frightened me more, but I didn't want to find out. Those first few hazy nights of us exchanging our deepest secrets as we curled up on the futon with a box of cookies flooded back to me. He didn't like the side effects of his medication; he threatened his mom he'd drink bleach. I gulped down a labored inhale so he wouldn't sense my fear, his cigarette smoke depriving my lungs of oxygen.

"I-I-I'm sorry," was all I had to offer. "I'll figure something out."

The apartment gods were looking out for me when I received a text from a friend. Her friend was looking to fill the closet-sized bedroom in her apartment immediately. I hopped right back on the subway across town less than thirty minutes after packing the makeup in my suitcase lest anyone knocked on my door to take it away.

"Hey girl!" Leanne greeted me with a warm smile. "Let me show you around."

Her belly ring and hipbones protruded from beneath her skin-tight yoga outfit as she sauntered around the penthouse suite. It was out of a women's magazine: marble counters, floor to ceiling windows, and a door of my own.

"This would be yours," she said, pointing to a generous excuse of a bedroom. Even at her size, she had to suck in to squeeze between the twin bed and the closet that connected directly to the foyer. It was perfect.

I couldn't tell you why I loved her immediately. But loving easily led to trouble, so I needed some form of screening process before I gave myself away to this new prospective roommate.

"OPI or Essie?" I asked. Without missing a beat, she offered a dissertation-level defense in support of OPI's superior formula, texture, and color variety.

I waited until midnight to return to my apartment, avoiding yet again that awkward song and dance with Gabe. As soon as he shut his bedside light, I threw the rest of my belongings into my suitcase and slept fully clothed beside it. The next morning, I awoke to a snowstorm with zero visibility, but knowing the dire nature of the situation, my dad's closest friend from college agreed to move me into the new penthouse suite anyway. Gabe couldn't know where I lived.

The tiny size of my new bedroom felt so in line with the journalist identity I chased. I was both at peace yet suffering. I was both free yet chained to my past.

I learned from my mistake at the advertising agency not to work on other projects while on the company's time. Now that I'd been let go, I had all the time in the world to pursue those paid opportunities I had let fall by the wayside in favor of that unpaid internship. They were mostly service articles, interviews, and reported features for the *Montreal Gazette* and *Reader's Digest*. I knew how to write those things with my eyes closed. But of course, I wouldn't be a true journalist if I didn't willingly submit myself to more suffering than I needed to. I flipped open that cigarette pack of joints, dying to light each and every last one of them like it was the eighth night of Chanukah.

Smoke swiveled freely throughout my windowless bedroom, but it managed to pry itself out from between a row of jackets and into the foyer like it had its own central nervous system. Maybe that's why I worshipped smoke. It didn't care what you wanted it to do. It weaved in and out at its leisure. It wrote inappropriate tweets. It called itself "freelance" journalist without giving an ounce of a fuck what you thought of it.

Because I was so high, it took me six hours to complete a freelance feature on winter-themed cardio exercises that would have otherwise taken me one. But it was nice to slow down. I had nowhere to be. I savored the time it took to write like I did the citrusy herbal taste of weed on my tongue. No one would be descending upon my bedroom door any time soon, the *clack, clack, clack* of almond-shaped nails on linoleum extracting me from my thought process.

Instead, the buzz of my phone—the phone I was definitely allowed to have beside me during the workday because I was my own boss—knocked me out of my blissful state.

New Text Message: Gabe

"Oh shit, oh shit, oh shit," I said out loud. He's plotting something. He found out where I live. He's outside the door with a gun. I told myself I wasn't going to read it. I buried my phone under a pile of laundry. Of course, that made me even more curious about what the message read.

"You forgot a blue pair of shoes," the text read.

I finally exhaled the secondhand smoke I had been holding in my lungs since I found him home alone in our apartment the day before. Sure, I was a true impostor at my job at the agency and in the women's magazine office. But I never felt more at home working from home.

Chapter 8

A DICK PIC SAYS A THOUSAND WORDS

He refuses to speak to me but it's so romantic that he likes my Instagram photos from seven years ago at 4:00 a.m.

—Millennial proverb

We all have a checklist. Sometimes it'll read, "Quinoa, zucchini, soy milk, and a secret stash of chocolate chips" for that bran muffin recipe I saw on *BuzzFeed* Tasty. Oh wait, wrong Post-It. Ah. There we go. We all have a checklist. Sometimes it'll read, "Loves to laugh, enjoys travel and moderate-to-high-intensity aerobic activity three times a week, and all the same Netflix shows as me." Other times it will read, "Wants two kids if we can afford it, has a healthy relationship with his parents, loves me more than I love myself, and is generally in love with love."

If you're smarter than me, which you are, duh, you can see why I set myself up for failure.

When I was twenty, I had been dating Jordan for an entire calendar year before he said I love you. "Why won't you say it?" I pressed like an emotional waffle iron against batter. "Is there something wrong with me? Is it because I have rolls on my stomach when I sit? Is it because my tweets aren't funny enough? Is it because my hair dries naturally as a Jew 'fro?"

"The more you press me to feel it, the more likely I never will," he said.

I asked these questions without a modicum of sarcasm because that's how damaging the denial of verbal—and written—love felt to me. I once made the mistake of writing for a highly trafficked blog about the time I first told him I loved him only to receive an "I opposite of hate you" in return, along with some other whiney complaints about how he didn't worship the ground I walked on enough. The article—admittedly unflattering for both of us—has either been taken down or switched to an anonymous author thanks to the really fun and pleasant death threats from fake emails I received from whom I can only imagine (and hope) were his friends. So don't waste your time searching for it and just keep your pretty little eyes peeled on me, or at least what I have to say. I matter. You matter. We're in this together.

When Jordan finally said the L Word (what am I, seven?) one cold December evening after we saw a terrible movie, it didn't feel like a reciprocation of affection but a stamp of approval that I desperately yearned for only so I could relay it to my group of friends, most of whom were already so deep into their monogamous relationships that I was already dubbed The Crazy Aunt among us. His delayed proclamation—after thirteen months of dating—made me feel as though I was a dog who'd been denied treats until she finally sat and offered her paw.

"Happy I finally dropped the L-bomb?" he teased.

I wouldn't have put it past him if he totally forgot what he'd said the day before and was instead referring to something that came out of his ass post-Indian buffet.

When we are denied of signifiers that mark the evolution of love, we feel the sharp yet virtually invisible pain of a paper cut we got crafting an unreciprocated Valentine's Day card. Why are we so quick to blame ourselves for these breaks in momentum, the feeling that not everything is fine all the time? If love was always perfect, our lives would be as bland as the first part of this sentence.

I think about all the traditional types of love I've received growing up: Valentine's Day cards and chocolate-covered marshmallows from my parents to warm my cold, dead heart; glittery cards adorning my locker once a year for every year of high school; an absurdly excessive amount of

Polish treats from my bubby because she doesn't want me to suffer the same level of loss she did as an orphan during the Holocaust. I come from a place of profound privilege in that I never felt lacking in love from my friends or family. I never questioned their love for me, although at more hormone-fueled times I wanted to. So why do men—a seemingly minute part of my life given that I wasn't allowed in a bedroom alone with them with the door closed until what feels like last week—so often have the power to rob me of my agency like a dementor in one of the Harry Potter books that Jordan read so I did, too?

My therapist might give me the cop-out answer of "You don't love yourself, blah blah blah," but that can't possibly be the case. I have a sister as a best friend, parents cooler than camp counselors who let you smoke weed in your cabin (they don't let me smoke weed but they do allow me to practice my most impressive swear words in front of them), and a group of friends who will accompany me to the ladies room to pee in the same stall and examine the diameters of our areolas. Here's the thing: feeling so overwhelmingly loved in all other facets of our lives only magnifies how devastating those tiny pockets of pseudo-love, noncompatibility, and even emotional abuse can feel when we don't have them.

And this is what happens next:

When you're so otherwise happy and content, a break in the so-called conventional love routine, no matter how small, is jarring to the system. It makes you crazy. It makes you think you aren't worthy of this person's love, or whatever the fuck it is that their Tinder profile happens to be advertising like a Kardashian endorsing hair vitamins. So here's a tip: instead of putting partners on pedestals, stop to think for a second that they love you—*are* loving you— the only way they know how. Perhaps their idea of love isn't PDA as you know and love it, but private displays of affection. Perhaps they don't need to Instagram the birthday cake you made them to taste how sweet it is. The way you want to be loved doesn't always align with the love they are ready to give you or are capable of giving you. And that's okay. You are capable of love and loving, and that in and of itself is a far more exciting option than its counterpart. Would you rather have loved and lost someone than to have never loved at all, or are you the reason shitty yet very true affirmations pervade my fucking Facebook timeline?

The truth is: I'm lucky.

I'm lucky things ended with Jordan, because I now have the foresight to know it's not him I was yearning for but my preconceived idea of love itself: a love I thought he could give me just because I was capable of it. I'm also lucky to have sat through *way* too many hours of his sporting events I didn't care about, while he limply waved to me from the pitcher's mound, throwing me a bone by telling me that he had "never" waved to anyone else while on the field before. *Great*, I thought, while sitting in the bleachers. *I might not be wifey material, but goddamn am I wavy material.* I'm lucky to have been dumped six times for girls with objectively shinier hair than me. Their Twitter accounts were all retweets of Gossip Girl quotes anyway, and I'm sure the two of them had tons more to talk about. I'm sure they got each other off waving to each other from the other side of the room.

Subtract this one human from the equation, and it confirms just how lucky I was to begin with. It wasn't just the marshmallows and glittery cards and *rugalach* that made me feel that way. (Material possessions can only get you so far in love, anyway, no matter what that Cartier bracelet might suggest.) It was—and is—my network of support that steps up to home plate when it's discovered that someone who convinced me to call him a boyfriend is actually sending other women ads on Craigslist, and to my knowledge, we never had a polyamory agreement (Yeah, I checked the Sent inbox. Like I said, a break in the love routine makes us ~Crazy~).

I may be the poster girl of the modern-day euphemism "We Receive the Love We Think We Deserve." And if that's you, too, I suggest you succumb to this truth bomb: you'll never feel okay about yourself if you continue to pit yourself against other women, other men, other writers, other scientists, other dancers, or other dental assistants. We will continue to find flaws in ourselves by using someone else's life as a litmus test to determine what feels good for us. In collectively convincing each other that we are some bullshit rendition of "Equal in the Eyes of God," we've made no room for individuality and owning up to our idiosyncrasies. You know, the unique traits that make us pretty fucking weird, but damn well deserving of the type of love that only the chick in the Philadelphia cream cheese commercial gets to experience. Sometimes, we are not meant to have shiny hair. We're meant to twirl our calloused fingers around salt-sprayed Jew 'fros while we contemplate the soaring analytics on our blogs.

I don't know what it's actually like to be in love, but I think of it as this: it feels like your heart is a *BuzzFeed* Tasty video of a cheese pull. Slow and satisfying, like your chest is permanently convulsing. I think of it as taking a strong bong hit. It'll make your gums tingle like you've just taken the residual cocaine off a bathroom toilet seat and applied it to the roots of your teeth. Not that I'd know what that's like, Mom. No siree. Not even that one time on Prince Arthur Street when I told you I was going to the library with Jenna.

"Sweetie, I think you're having a stroke," said my most recent boyfriend, Noah.

The thing about Noah is that even when he was mad at me, he called me Sweetie. There was no "Marissa Iris Rozen Miller, explain yourself this instant!" It was always "Sweetie! What did I tell you about going between my butt cheeks? Only the cheeks!" It sounds cheeky on paper, but there was real wrath in his eyes (and a fear-induced clenched asshole).

When you love someone, you are biologically unable to feel anything but an overarching love feeling even during objectively trying times. Like when one of you transgresses the "no butt stuff" rule.

Shout-out to Roxane Gay, but sorry not sorry if qualifying falling in love as my biggest accomplishment makes me a Bad Feminist. Falling in love says less about the other person and more about myself. In previous relationships, partners defined my self-worth. Slap my ass and call me sad did 'n' single if I were ever caught dead swiping my youth away in a meager attempt at finding a suitor. Nothing made me feel more pathetic than being alone and going to serious lengths to rectify that. Had a boyfriend I could send my first essay drafts to even though they had never so much as read baseball stats? Sign me the fuck up. Late to my own Passover Seder because my date had to chug a beer in the middle of the street before meeting my family? Heck, yeah. Boyfriends were accessories to my self-esteem, glimmering and on display yet never fitting quite right on the mannequin. I hated them all, or at least I grew to hate them, eventually, but they were a means to an end. (One time the back end. Let's not talk about that. At least not here. Maybe later.)

I've said I love you to probably every boyfriend I ever had. My high school administration preached sexual abstinence, but never did any authority figure—mother, father, teacher, or swim coach—teach me how to *not* give all my love away. L-word abstinence felt like an awkward void. How do you hang up the phone? How do you wish them a safe flight when they fly back to their hometown? What do you say when you turn off the lights and go to bed? I've said it so many times to people I couldn't care less about that the first time I meant it, I felt like I had run through my quota already, like it was hollow and empty and didn't mean anything. Like when Samantha in *Sex and the City* is worried she's no longer able to orgasm because half of New York's population has already made her uterus ricochet against her pelvis, or something like that. I'm not a fucking doctor, but you know what I mean.

I once heard Usher, bless his underrated-but-never-forgotten soul, say that he's in love with love. I get it. You're chasing a high, if not the D. (Dopamine. Gosh, don't be gross!). If you previously felt like an empty, hollow, worthless excuse of a human shell (hi!), to be in love is to self-actualize. But if you've—gasp—mended areas of your life that are holding you back from feeling like the biggest boss that anyone's seen thus far (for starters, have the ability to be in public without having to hyperventilate into a plastic bag—also hi!), then love isn't so much about completing an incomplete life but complementing an existing full one. Not in a way that the waiter will send over a free shitty flan cake when it's your "birthday" at 3 Amigos and you're hiding day-four hair under a sombrero. But in a way that the mixologist, *NOT* the bartender, will send over absinthe cocktails that are on fire and very sweet and made with Grey Goose—not that Polar Ice bullshit you stole from the SAQ when you were fourteen. He respects you and you both made each other laugh when you were waiting for a table (you're a solid and respectable seven out of ten on the cute scale so you had to wait, you peasant, you!). But under the flame of those cocktails your skin glows. It's a spa day. You feel, oh god, don't say it. Saying it. Ah, it's happening. Beautiful. And despite the pervasive rhetoric that forces women to downplay how fantastic they feel about themselves—aesthetically and otherwise—you can't help but admit you are worthy of this joy.

Mixologist Man isn't buying your love, you see. He's a metaphor for setting your life on fire (don't worry, your apartment is still intact. Free Flan Cake Man is nice, convenient, makes you feel wanted. That's okay when you haven't Figured Your Shit Out Yet, Which Is Okay, Because Neither Have I But I Can Now Officially Pretend So Well I Might Not Even Be Pretending). Free flan is the easy way to feel. But drinks on fire? Oh god. This is how I felt when I met Noah for the second time.

I'll get to that. Just let me splash a little water on my face and rub the kinks out of my neck.

The first time we met doesn't count because he doesn't remember it. I was seventeen and he was twenty-four and he was wearing a white Fruit of the Loom T-shirt at a mutual friend's backyard party. He had not one but two cartilage piercings side by side (BOLD CHOICE. MUST BANG). There were green Converse sneakers to top off the look in case you're not convinced I was capable of objectifying a handsome man, because fuck the patriarchy. (Literally, fuck it. I'll wait. But use a condom or make sure your NuvaRing is lodged far enough up there. Personally would not recommend it, though. I would know because NuvaRings + working as a dancer at a Jewish sleepaway camp means you might have to explain to a gap-toothed seven-year-old that no, that is not a glow stick prize for doing the YMCA real good.)

I knew Noah tangentially through friends, or maybe even the People You May Know section of Facebook. My opening line was:

"Hi, do you know Jennifer?"

"Yeah, she's my sister."

End scene.

V-neck had heard through a mutual friend that I was interested in writing for the school newspaper. He posted on my wall asking me to write for him, which is the modern-day equivalent of a marriage proposal on the Jumbotron.

"Come to my office to pitch me ideas," he then sent over Facebook chat after I gave him a curt "Will do" in response to his wall post. *From my limited knowledge of how article pitching works, you typically rely on a paper trail to the tune of email*, I thought.

If you're excited about a soon-to-be softcore porn scene where "pitch me ideas" is code for "perform fellatio on me," I'm giving you seven minutes to go ahead and rub one out if you didn't get the chance to get off a few paragraphs ago, because I'm sorry to say this is far from spank bank material unless you get off on a pathetic teen auditioning for the part of unpaid student reporter.

"I don't have any ideas. I've only written angry poetry before," I replied. "Oh, actually, my dad has a client who is a sustainable farmer. Maybe I can talk to him," I said, feeling far more confident in front of a screen where we were solidifying story ideas than I did face-to-face with him in the hallway.

A few weeks later, I filed a story that was neither fully reported nor coherent. I had this beautiful Jewish demigod tell me he was unable to run my story because "sources need to go on record in order for this to qualify as journalism."

Self-esteem = shattered.

Nether regions = 1,000 percent chance of precipitation.

End scene.

Allow me to reiterate that objectifying men or reducing them to the level of infatuation I have for them is not a scintillating literary device but a coping mechanism to lament the fallen soldiers, not who failed to fall for me but who failed to fall for me the way I wanted them to.

My relationship with Noah would later be relegated to Facebook chat and infrequent university hallway sightings. Time masked the sting of rejection, where images of his too-tall frame towering over me only moments before walking away were replaced by men my own size who asked me to read my poetry out loud to them, which, let's be honest, is the equivalent of masturbating while admiring yourself in the mirror. Some of them took wardrobe cues from high-end men's magazines, but none of them unabashedly wore a mean pair of beat-up Chucks quite like Noah did well past his midthirties.

I know this because he wore a similar pair—this time black—to grab a friendly drink one late fall evening in 2014 at Honey Martin's pub in Montreal's *Notre-Dame-de-Grâce* borough. It had been four years since we first met, and two years since we'd seen each other last. Our voices competed for volume as we dissected the intellectual merits of the porn features we had both simultaneously been writing for the same major magazine at the time. He didn't pay for my two glasses of red wine. I didn't receive any tangible signifiers of affection I had so fondly paraded at the top of my checklist. I forgot about my usual need for praise or an onslaught of tipsy texts when we were apart. I wasn't skeptical of his intentions when he asked to continue the conversation at his apartment nearby over another bottle of wine. I declined not because I was worried about what he'd think of me if I agreed but because I was allergic to his cat and didn't have any antihistamines on me.

"Marissa, I'm so nervous right now," he said as we walked out the pub's door.

"What happened? Are you on a tight deadline? Are the cops after you?"

"I just wanted to kiss you all night and, I mean, I don't know if—" he stammered like he was defending his master's thesis.

What the actual . . .

"Alright, bring it in, buddy," I said, motioning him toward me like a coach summoning his football players into a pregame huddle.

I trembled all the way home, grazing my lips with my cold fingers to make sure they were still there. The kiss was strong and deliberate. It was real and it was felt, and all that remains is its memory.

Chapter 9

CRIME AND PUNISHMENT

I opened my palms, feeling the cool crunch of the candy bag in my hands. A woman I had never seen before handed it to me with a half-smile. Her eyes were small atop a nose dotted with a ski-hill mogul. Her jowls fell from her jawbone. Faded chestnut dye coated only the tips of her hair, revealing a crown of salt-and-pepper tufts like a rabbi's beard.

"Thought you might like these," she said, her voice high pitched and raspy at the same time.

I didn't mind that she was trying to make small talk with me and my sister. After all, we had been sitting on our grandfather's couch for the last forty-five minutes with empty, gurgling bellies as the rest of our family finished exchanging pleasantries. It always took what felt like forever to migrate to the dining room table for the Passover Seder. This stranger was someone else to look at, something else to think about. Someone else to acknowledge my existence when I felt like an insignificant fourteen-year-old, my sister only a couple years younger.

"I didn't know anything about you guys, so I figured I'd go with lollipops," she continued. My sister and I wordlessly glanced at each other as if to say, *You're right. You don't know a thing about us. Who are you and why are you here?*

"Thanks," I said.

I glanced down at the bag, the dollar store tag imprinted on its bright pink label. There was no *Kosher for Pesach* sign on it, but she couldn't have known. The gesture gave me arrhythmia. The good kind, if there was one.

After my dad beckoned us to the long chestnut dining table, I lathered my hands with my Zaidie's seashell-shaped soap reserved for guests. I was very much a guest in his house. I wasn't at the point—and never would be, I would later accept—where I could throw a weekend bag down on his couch and jump on it like I was in a Downy fabric softener commercial as most grandchildren got to do with their grandparents during the holidays, or when their parents went out of town for the night, mostly Burlington, Vermont, for limited-edition American snacks from Trader Joe's. I had my maternal bubby for that, who lived a six-minute drive away near the Cavendish Mall. Alright, enough pondering my family dynamics as I wash my hands, I thought. This counted as, like, seven *netilat yadayim* rituals.

Catching a glimpse of my profile in the mirror, I froze. The mogul, the matted hair, and when I had the courage to face myself head-on, the small eyes. All that was missing were the jowls I had the joy of looking forward to when I reached her age that teetered somewhere between late thirties and early forties, and the salt-and-pepper tufts of curly hair that bounced when she laughed.

"Mammas, how thrilled are we to have your auntie Tammy join us tonight?" my dad said as he put his arm around the stranger when I returned to the living room. She looked amused the moment she heard her brother address his two children as "mammas," but it was something we had come to accept the way it's best to pierce ears or perform circumcisions—both religious and medical—on a child when they are too young to know any better. We were conditioned to never question the institutions that governed us, and so the name just stuck.

"Yeah, we're so happy to have you at our Seder," I said. "Hope you like copious amounts of food and dragging out the Haggadah reading." I couldn't tell if I was easing or tightening the tension.

I had heard tales about Tammy in the way I did about Costa the creepy night watchman at Y Country Camp every summer. Given all the cautionary tales my father told me about her in passing growing up, I never thought I'd end up in the same room as her. There was that one time she had been standing on the corner of St. Jacques and Elmhurst soliciting clients passing by and instantly cowered when she realized it was my father in the black sedan, my day-care-aged sister and me bundled up in one-piece snowsuits strapped to car seats. There was her several-month sentence at a women's prison in Joliette, Quebec, for a crime that sounded too convoluted for me to understand when I learned about it in my early teens. These were all stories my father had either disclosed to me in a Freudian slip of a trance, or that I had heard him discuss with my mother in hushed tones. But the more snippets of information I picked up about her, the more I demanded to learn.

* * *

I didn't have the language to articulate that The Truth™, no matter how upsetting, never scared me. All those years watching *Trauma: Life in the ER* on TLC during pedagogical days numbed my ability to feel any real sense of disgust or disdain. This numbness extended to my everyday life. By my parents hiding who my aunt was from me, my curiosity about her festered like the termites I saw on TLC's wounded patients. But, according to my parents, I was always too young to know exactly what kind of lifestyle she led. I knew I'd be eligible for my driver's license at age sixteen and my first legal drink at eighteen. But there were other rites of passage that never quite fit neatly into small boxes, so it was up to me to seek the truth on my own terms.

I watched as Tammy cracked a slice of chocolate-covered matzah in half and took a big, triumphant bite. Even when she smiled, her big gap teeth two keys on a Steinway, she looked mischievous, even guilty.

"Tam, what did I tell you?" my dad asked with a mocking scolding tone only older brothers are biologically designed to pull off. "You can't have that stuff with your diabetes."

She retorted that she'd be fine. Of course she'd be fine. The woman had nine lives, I heard my mom once say under her breath.

My perverse fascination with my aunt would have worried my dad had he known the extent of it. So, following that fateful Passover Seder, I kept our Hotmail email exchanges private. She has one tattoo, but only I know where it is. Oh look, her dealer arrived, she's so sorry, but she has to go. Her roommate is being an asshole and stole money from her, so this might not end well. She would love to talk to me some other time. No problem, Auntie Tammy! Talk soon. I logged out of my account with the type of smile that only follows after doing something wrong.

I was so young only a handful of years had passed since my Bat Mitzvah. And yet my concern was her approval, something you'd have to earn from a cooler, more experienced older sister. A Designated Cool Female, if you will. Never had a family member addressed me like I was anything but a child. She was real, and if "Real recognize real," then, well, you do the math.

For the next eight years, my father invited her to every extravagant Jewish high holiday dinner my mom hosted in our home. He felt he owed her that much—another chance to be a part of a family. She was done with crime and she had reformed, he said. She had locked down a job at JEM Workshop, known as Jewish Employment Montreal, which provides career opportunities to those struggling with either intellectual or physical disabilities. And even if she didn't reform in a traditional enough sense to appease my family's conservative-leaning sensibilities, I would have accepted her the way she accepted me.

I always took that thirty-five-minute pocket after dinner and before dessert to steal away from the long chestnut dining room table into a corner with Tammy. It was our chance to fill in the gaps her dealer left when he knocked on her door mid-dial-up-internet exchange. Like meeting a biological parent for the first time long after being adopted into and raised by another family, it was too late in the game to each fulfill our traditional aunt-niece roles, so we caught up like old friends.

She'd regale me with stories about dropping acid at age eleven in her childhood kitchen, the kaleidoscope of shapes and colors dancing in her eyes and causing her to choke on her laughter in front of her mother, my late bubby. There was the story about ripping the toilet seats out of her elementary school bathroom "just to see what would happen," and having the cops kick down her door while she was in the midst of manufacturing illicit substances in her kitchen with the intention to distribute. Everything she told me about herself took place so long ago I couldn't fathom how she remembered it all, or why she even chose to. Surely, she had experienced something adult-like within the last week or two, like she had found a great sale on cherries or had her sink fixed—not a guide on the specific type of reggae that pairs best with each strand of weed like an addict's wine and cheese. Had she actually gotten clean? Or were we deluding ourselves into thinking so? What did it mean to cherish a life you were programmed to escape?

The juxtaposition of sitting in front of a half-eaten Seder plate while learning about the intricacies of the Montreal drug trade was equal parts thrilling and terrifying. But had I learned about her earlier, I wouldn't have had an insatiable curiosity to lead me down this gruesome rabbit hole. Like a *Trauma: Life in the ER* binge on a Tuesday afternoon.

* * *

"Here, can you get this?" I asked my friend Chelsea, motioning for her to tighten my skinny spaghetti straps hooked onto a satin black corset. Both of my hands were full as I painted and erased a flick of cat-eye eyeliner over and over again until its gentle smile of a parabola created a Tyra Banks–approved smize pointing squarely toward my temples. I always cared about being pretty, what I looked like. But this time it really mattered. We were four minutes away from waddling on stiletto heels into a cab bound for Prince Arthur, a pedestrian-friendly cobblestone street dotted with bars too dark to spot counterfeit IDs.

After the two months of summer camp ended, it was tradition for all fourteen-year-olds or counselors-in-training (known as CITs) to congregate on the bustling street. Swapping our cotton Soffe shorts for Miss Sixty jeans that hit just above the pubic bone, it was our long-awaited chance to show our fellow campers what we looked like—and who we were—when our Abercrombie tank tops weren't covered in actual mud.

My summer with Chelsea had been perfect so far, so I put an immense amount of pressure on myself to keep it that way: I managed to not gain any weight despite an onslaught of soft-baked chocolate chip cookies at my disposal at all times; my boyfriend wrote me hand-written letters every day while we were both at camp; and I promised every camper who went to bed on time that they'd get a braid, pigtails, or a hairstyle of their choosing the following day. Unsurprisingly, the cabin fell silent at 9:00 p.m. flat every night.

When we paid our cab fare and spilled onto the cobblestone streets of *Plateau-Mont-Royal*, Chelsea's boyfriend, Greg, greeted us with a mix of my bunkmates and classmates. It was my first time ever setting foot in "adult" territory, so I let Greg lead the way. He was an entire year older, so that naturally meant he had a lifetime's worth of experience over me.

I felt wholly overdressed as we huddled into a side street alley and sat down on the gravel littered with beer caps and grocery receipts. My massive red fake designer purse from Canal Street contained nothing but a Nokia flip phone, fake

ID, and debit card, so I placed all three in my bra and sat on my bag like a makeshift picnic blanket. The appletinis and dance floors I was promised were nowhere in sight.

Despite having no backpack or oversized pockets, Greg unearthed a glass apparatus the size of a pitcher's forearm. He expertly lit one end with a lighter and lifted the massive tube to his mouth, inhaling, holding it in while looking furtively around our circle of friends, then exhaling a gust of smoke so opaque it concealed his freckles, green eyes, and Buddha belly poking out of his Led Zeppelin T-shirt/button-down combo. The conversation oscillated from camp to school to hookups and back to school again. I wasn't going to be the first to insert an amateur hour question about what the actual fuck was going on.

Before I could display any sign of protest, the phallic, bulbous tube was in my lap. Lest anything fall out (its hundred screws or pillow of ash in the bowl, for example), I held it like I was picnicking with an overstuffed Subway sandwich. When Greg lit the end for me, I inhaled as if aiming to flood my circulatory system with oxygen, the type of deep, performative inhale that propelled me onto piano recital stages and public speaking podiums in moments of debilitating fear. It was a shocking sensation, like chugging a glass of vodka when you thought it was water.

"That's my bitch!" Chelsea said, cheering me on. I took three more hits, letting the dry heat ignite every cell in my body.

As the bong made its rounds throughout the circle, my legs unfolded themselves and began to walk away. My heels felt higher, my jeans felt tighter, and my breasts tickled as an unanswered phone buzzed away in my bra. My only explanation for what was happening to me was that I was actually trapped in a game of the Sims and the green plumbob above my head controlling my every move was, in fact, a brick of weed.

Three or thirty minutes—who's to say—into walking away from the alley, my classmate Jeremy caught up to me, and the gang followed closely behind. A sigh of relief came over me as I spotted familiar faces in the dark, which my peripheral vision now painted an even murkier hue. Each stiletto-lined step I took got lodged deeper and deeper into the crevice of a cobblestone, making my already turtle-slow gait even harder to watch from afar without grimacing. After, again, three or thirty minutes of walking—who's to say!—we landed in a leather-clad booth in a brightly lit La Belle Province hot dog chain.

"Excuse me, Jeremy, but have you seen my hands?" I asked, poking him in the cheek as if to inspect the doughy flesh encasing his jaw.

"They're right there," he motioned, clearly humoring me.

"I have no idea what you're talking about," I said.

He placed his hands upon mine—aha! There they were—and held them together between his, like I was a child who lost their mittens playing outside in the snow. I knew weed was supposed to make you relax, but no one warned me I'd forget how to fucking locate and operate my own limbs.

I willed myself to grab his water bottle, holding it like a baby who had just found their hands for the first time. Instead of taking a sip like I intended, I poured it over my head and down my body like I was enacting a Dasani-sponsored ALS Ice Bucket Challenge.

Lest I drown my brick of a phone in a puddle of bottled water and tears, I dislodged it from my bra. And that's when it hit me. I needed to get the fuck out of here before my trip went to a very, very bad place.

Before Chelsea could talk me out of it, I was dialing my dad's number and listening to the sound of his voice say "Huh-llo?" after the first ring. He was an answer-on-the-first-ring type of guy, even during peak tax season. His voice was so soothing I didn't want to ruin it with my news.

"Hi, Dad? What are you doing?"

"Ah, you know, some standard Saturday night accounting. What's up, pretty?"

"Um, can you get me?"

"Everything okay?"

"Um, I, um, no."

"What did you do?"

The guy spiralled for six days if he didn't get his dressing on the side. There was no way I could tell him I did drugs in a dark alley and now feel like I might be stuck in a Salvador Dali painting.

"I did a thing and I don't know how to make it go away," I managed, looking down at my hands that, thanks to muscle memory, I had used to miraculously place this terrifying phone call.

I wanted to believe my dad's click of the receiver after our punctuated call was a telepathic "Say no more, fam." But I instantly felt a sense of failure knowing I did the one thing I wasn't supposed to do. Enough overanalyzing. I'd find out soon enough what he really thought.

I put on my best "not high" face when he pulled up. But, like tripping on drugs and holding in a laugh like Auntie Tammy did in her kitchen high on acid around her mother, I only looked guiltier.

"So? Start talking," he said with a sinister tone I hadn't heard since that time my sister and I, at age five and three, respectively, thought it would be a kind gesture to carve our names on the passenger door of his Honda, dotting the I's in our name with hearts.

"I'm really sorry. I didn't mean to," I said.

"What do you mean, 'You didn't mean to'? Did you fall face first onto drugs and breathe in at the right time?"

"It wasn't planned or anything. I was supposed to just walk around and see old friends, and then it happened," I said.

"That's how a life of addiction and crime starts. That's how Tammy started," he reminded me unhelpfully.

It was as if her name had become synonymous with a "bad path"—or more aptly, a dark alley littered with bottle caps, grocery store receipts, and lost teens. But she was more than her wrongdoings. She wasn't exactly my role model in the way Baby Spice was, how I thought about showing up to Emma Bunton's house in Liverpool and wearing her peach skin as a spring-friendly coat. But Tammy was a figure I looked up to in a different way, a way that didn't make me feel, for once, entirely like a sack of garbage left out in the sun. I didn't need to proverbially crane my neck to get a glimpse of her on a pedestal. She was on my level in a way my dad would never understand—and in turn, she saw me on hers.

I rested my head on the pillow that night rocking uncomfortably back and forth to the beat of the spinning sensation in my head. The transition to sleep was seamless. There was little difference between the bad dream in which I lived and the one I visited when I fell asleep.

* * *

It was so windy that, had my mom not been wearing a hip-hugging pencil skirt from the sale section at Ann Taylor Loft, she would have reenacted a Marilyn Moment right in the middle of Queen Mary Road, a pulse of life in an otherwise uneventful part of town called Hampstead. I should have been serenading her with lines about how everything would be okay, I'm a good kid I promise, I'm not a fuckup at all, but all I could think was *Fuck, how am I going to light my joint later in all this goddamn wind?* And if there was any moment in my eighteen-year-old existence I could have used a hit, it would have been then.

My mom shifted her eyes awkwardly in each direction hoping that no one would notice her as we descended the steep steps to the rehab center. My dad trailed behind us with his hands lodged in his pockets, hanging his head in shame. In this type of situation, my sister and I would normally have held hands as we do when we're escorting each other to the bathroom in a crowded bar or leaving T.J. Maxx giddily with five hundred dollars' worth of second-tier designer purses we paid fifty dollars for. But any form of solidarity would have confirmed our complicity in this thing we'd both been accused of called "using drugs."

A rabbi masquerading as an addiction counselor stood up to greet my family, extending a limp arm to shake only my father's hand. I sat down on the cold plastic chair feeling exposed, large, wrong, and weird, not unlike the chair that made me feel exposed, large, wrong, and weird sitting next to my crush Alex in fifth grade when he didn't want to be my Yiddish folk song dance partner.

"I understand we're having some family issues," the rabbi began, crossing his legs and leaning back in his chair. "Who would like to start?"

My sister and I shot each other a knowing glance as if to say, "Dude, I'm not saying shit, and also can we get Starbucks after this nonsense?"

My dad, ever the camp counselor, took the lead. He explained that we were here because of a history of severe addiction on his side of the family and given that it's both a genetic and environmental trait, he was worried his daughters were exhibiting "all the signs."

"What kind of signs?" the rabbi shot back.

"I think the real driving factor is that four years ago, Marissa smoked weed even though we told her never to touch it. She swore up and down—wait, sorry, that's a

Christian thing—she promised that she wouldn't do it again. And what do you know? We find a lighter in Michelle's pocket a few weeks ago, and it just raises some questions about what they're doing together."

"What kind of questions does it raise exactly, Mr. Miller?"

"All kinds of things," my dad said. "Like, how long have they been doing it? How often? With whom? How do we parent children we can't trust? How do we come to terms with the fact that kids will experiment with dangerous things? How do we sit back and let them harm themselves? How could I ever live with myself if something catastrophic were to happen to them?"

I thought about my inability to find my hands in a diner. That was about as catastrophic as it gets when you're high on weed, I thought. That, or bingeing on Cheetos and feeling fat after, which I conceded would be my personal hell, but still.

"Ah, yes. You ask the million-shekel questions," said the rabbi.

I was too busy watching his ashy beard bob up and down when he spoke to register the contents of his stream of consciousness, but the gist was this: the Talmud doesn't condone drug use due to any potential sinning that may arise from it, like theft or violence. And while he couldn't pat me on the back for smoking a joint and refraining from robbing a bank at gunpoint, what he could do was sell me on sobriety. So what if I wasn't allowed to pray when I'm high? So what if I wasn't allowed to perform legal, political, or religious functions when my brain was far more wired to pick my split ends while watching *Pineapple Express*? Unless you consider the first sip of iced cold Diet Coke after a particularly harsh doobie a religious function, I wanted no part in his weed-free world.

Getting treatment from someone decked out in full rabbi gear felt as misplaced as open-heart surgery from a clown that fashions giraffes out of balloons at kids' birthday parties. It wasn't until he led us to his wife's office, an accredited social worker, that my ears perked up.

A thick, blonde *sheitel* framed her shiny forehead. Her skin would have otherwise been post-Zamboni ice-rink smooth had it not been for two deep smile lines sandwiching her thin lips like a pair of skis. I saw only a whisper of her wrist, a fleshy slab of meat that only contributed to her air of maternal and professional authority.

"What you need to understand about drug dependence," she continued after a few moments of pleasantries, "is that often it is a symptom of an untreated mental illness, like depression or anxiety. We need to talk about those conditions as possible driving factors."

It was the first time I felt like I could relate to those two words beyond "Ugh, I'm so depressed I failed my math test," and "Ew, I'm having so much anxiety over my hair today." But I let those words linger in the air like weed smoke, watching them undulate in my mind the way shapes begin to form against the blacks of your eyelids when you shut them too tightly.

I left the rehab center holding a folder full of antidrug brochures in Hebrew, yet I was also armed with more questions than answers. Do I have a mental illness? What's wrong with me? Will treatment hurt even more than the illness itself? Am I legally mandated to seek treatment, or can I continue to be broken within the confines of my own identity, my privacy? Can I continue to smoke weed as long as I promise not to rob any banks?

My sweet parents, God bless their souls, assumed that one session could fix me and my sister for good. And I so wanted that to be true. But nothing changed—not the friends I hung out with in dark alleys, the low-slung Miss Sixty jeans I wore, or the weed I smoked. If I pretended that session never happened, maybe I could avoid any further treatment and any potential diagnosis that arose from it. I wanted to plead ignorant, confused, young, weird. As Jews, my nuclear and extended family alone have enough physical ailments to pose as rashy and bloated subjects in a medical textbook. And yet the term "mental illness" never came up after that fateful session. Not once. Until Tammy died.

"There are lots of things I'm learning about her, even now as I'm handling her estate," my dad said in the weeks following her death.

I had found out via FaceTime when I was holed up in a hostel in Vietnam. Her kidneys had failed, one of the many complications she experienced after years of drug use. I know there's never a "right" time to die, but after all those times I waited for her to log online to chat, the least she could have done was hung on a couple more days to exchange one last fist bump with me after I flew back from the other side of the world. But this wasn't about me or my selfish need for closure.

"Like what? What are you learning about her?" I asked, placing my chin on the back of my hand at his kitchen table.

"Well, she basically had no money to her name, so the financial aspect isn't particularly complicated," he said, flipping through a wad of files. "But you know, I'm pretty surprised the nurses at the Jewish General Hospital never told me she had a personality disorder. That could have changed some things."

I was approaching twenty-four years old by this point, and well-versed enough in mental health issues both from reporting on them extensively and experiencing them first-hand that I had known this to be true. That having a deeper look into her psyche could have allowed us to see not just the fragments of her that frightened us but help explain the choices she made. We derided her for doing drugs as if it were necessarily her own doing, or specifically, her own choosing. To me, self-medicating a mental illness made as much sense as dipping your entire body into a frozen lake when you can't shake a burning fever. We aren't designed to prevail through discomfort, no matter how resilient our loving mothers remind us to be. Finding refuge even in our vices doesn't make us bad people. We are not the drugs we do, the low-slung Miss Sixty pants we wear, nor the friends who pressure us into participating in cool teen rites of passage. We're the sum of our parts. The same way Tammy will always be a part of mine.

Chapter 10

OPEN CARRY

There's pain like childbirth, which pierces so deeply evolution grants new mothers amnesia as a way to encourage them to keep procreating. Then, there's pain that stays with you the rest of your life. Darwin is not on our side for this one.

"Fuck," I said at the dinner table four bites into my burrito. "So that's what that was," I said, pulling away from Cassidy's phone.

The Hansel and Gretel trail of blood running from my inner thighs down to my calloused feet wasn't a bad period, nor were the Maraschino cherry–thick clumps stuck to my skin like leeches.

"We'd been trying for about a month now," Cassidy said, "and I just had this excruciating pain as I sat down on the toilet. It all came gushing out."

I nodded in agreement, furtively pulling up a photo I found on Google that looked eerily similar to what I had experienced four years before, four hours before running my first half-marathon. It was the Googling I hadn't been able to do during the fact since my fingers trembled and trickled with sweat no matter how hard I tried to grip onto my phone. Onto something, anything, that felt real.

"Look, I'm no doctor," Cassidy said, "but that to me, given all your symptoms, is a miscarriage."

A flurry of conflicting thoughts swiveled through my brain. First, I had been twenty-three. Miscarriages don't *happen* to people in their early twenties. If it wasn't discussed in an issue of *Cosmo*, my Bible, it couldn't possibly apply to me in any real way. Second, my copper IUD deemed over 99 percent effective meant there was no way I could have been pregnant. Third, my rage toward my OB-GYN for not listening to me, for evacuating me out of his office like the contents of an ostomy bag when I so much as asked for an ultrasound to detect the correct placement of said IUD, was far stronger than the grief I had toward the loss of life that could have been.

We're taught to perform emotions like acts of a play: we hate our partners if we don't flail our arms in hysterics once they get down on one knee; we necessarily think a bride is hideous if our jaws don't drop to the floor when she emerges in her white dress for the first time; we hate our friend and the life they created if we don't instantly stick out our tongue and pinch their newborn's cheeks upon meeting them. These were rules I had learned by watching other women, reading about other women, studying other women, and yearning to be like other women. My miscarriage discovery was no different. When you learn you miscarried a child, you're a baby killer if you don't immediately break down.

Cassidy, along with our two other friends, looked at me expectantly. I felt like I owed them a speech, a toast barely audible through sobs, a performance to confirm their preconceived ideas about what someone who has suffered through a miscarriage is supposed to look like. But nowhere in my psychological user manual was there a how-to on coping with trauma when experiencing it through the cataracts of hindsight. Was there a chapter in said manual explaining how to be sad about something I didn't realize was happening to me until years later? Was I a bad person if, for once, I wasn't sad at all?

I continued to chew on my burrito like nothing had happened, the irony of its fleshy mess dripping from my cheek not lost on me.

By this point, I was a pro at living with trauma years after the fact. Learning I was raped only after the Harvey Weinstein trial made this retrospective miscarriage discovery feel all too familiar. While it was happening, and for the subsequent seven years, I carried my rape with me as an unwanted sexual advance, not a crime, but something that happens to women just because. I continued to live my life just as I had before the rape, jogging alone at night and flirting with strange men in bars. I wasn't by any means a "model rape victim," the type magazines teach you how to support in times of need and weakness. But that didn't undermine my experience any less. It just prepared me for other experiences we so rarely talk about that many of us don't even realize they're happening.

As I licked the last bits of burrito off my fingertips, I felt consumed with guilt for not having lost my appetite at the site of those gory images that, four years ago, spilled through the mesh lining of my magenta Lululemon shorts. I wasn't about to break out into theatrics to make the stories of my life easier for others to digest. Instead, I felt ravenous with curiosity about how my body would test me next.

Chapter 11

BAD BRIDE

I felt like Moses parting the sea as I walked down the aisle of crisp white dresses, each inch of wall covered in tulle.

On Instagram, the dresses hadn't seemed this intimidating. In the pictures, models on my Explore page and acquaintances on my feed gazed wistfully out into the distance as sweetheart necks framed their Sephora-sample highlighted collarbones. Their heads were thrown back in fake-laughs while their tousled manes grazed their exposed backs. Umm, hello. That level of choreography went down literally every time I needed to take a new display picture. I could do that. I could gaze. I could laugh. I could be a bride just like them.

I collected pictures of dresses dating back four years, but forgot what they all looked like once it came time to choose them at the bridal boutique. I tried to conjure my stack of magazine cutouts, unable to recall not what *Vanity Fair* said about the dress itself but how thin the model was who wore it.

Did they say backless is out and embellishments are in? Or is it the other way around? Fuck.

The store clerk pointed at several options she thought would flatter my shape, pressing gently on each contender like Vanna White revealing hidden letters on an episode of *Wheel of Fortune.* I nodded in half-hearted agreement, so she hung them up in my changing room. I slipped into an ivory trumpet gown with bulky sleeves that gave my shoulders the appearance of snow globes.

It was a costume, for all intents and purposes. This wasn't me. Where were the ripped and frayed hems? The leather? The colors that don't match?

Before I could consent, Russian-speaking seamstresses pulled and prodded at my waist and chest. I was either too busty or not busty enough. I was always too short. Nothing about the experience made me want to throw my head back and laugh. Except for, maybe, the idea of unironically playing dress-up as a twenty-four-year-old.

"I'm hungry and I want sushi," I said to my sister, mom, and bubby, who were the only people in my circle I felt comfortable burdening with my narcissistic look-at-me-in-a-wedding-dress shopping trip. Naturally, I hadn't eaten that day, and feeding my most basic human need for food trumped finding a dress my guests would approve of. Or that I would approve of. Only a Good Bride would have gone through the whole song and dance of slipping fifty different dresses over her lithe, empty body, and walking out of there with a gown she couldn't help but admire and show off.

"Well, there's still one you haven't tried," the seamstress reminded me. She lifted up a dress similar in silhouette to the problematic first one. This time, it dipped lower down my cleavage, squeezing my breasts together to resemble a Brazilian Butt Lift after photo.

Every second sequin glimmered against the doily-esque lace. The back, featuring approximately six thousand buttons, required two women working from both ends just to fasten it shut. I wasn't only thrilled because it cost seven hundred dollars—about a grand less than the shop's other offerings—but it was a sample size plucked straight off the mannequin. It didn't matter what I looked like when I walked down the aisle, when I posed for pictures in front of the synagogue, or when I was hoisted onto a chair in the middle of the dance floor while I waved a pink napkin over my head like a lasso. It mattered that my dress physically fit neatly within the prototype of what a perfect woman should look like or weigh. And if I walked into the reception hall with the sneaking suspicion that I was perfect on a physical level, maybe I could weasel my way into feeling confident enough to eat an appetizer, or even look back on my wedding day fondly. To feel confident, it's a lot easier to remember a single digit size in my head than to recite mantras I heard on a podcast.

When I was a teenager, my dad had me perform the "pencil test" every time I left the house to make sure my clothes covered enough skin when I bent down to pick something up. Mid-speeches after the wedding ceremony, I thought to myself that I should have had him at the bridal boutique to remind me to pick up a pencil in this wedding dress before buying it—I would have learned before it was too late that its inner corset lining was made of steel beams, and it would puncture a kidney if I tried to so much as take a full breath.

My mom, dad, and sister set their alarms for 7:30 a.m. so they could jump on me while blasting "Marry You" by Bruno Mars. I felt crowded given that they were piled onto my childhood twin-sized bed. It was a thing they did every year on my birthday when I lived at home, so enacting it on my wedding day, of all days, made me feel like more of a daughter than a wife.

"Who's ready to roll, bitch?!" one or all of them exclaimed. I was too groggy to determine which one of them said it. It could have been anyone's guess.

"Me," I said, mustering every drop of leftover caffeine in my circulatory system to appear perky and actually stoked about this fancy school play I was about to put on for an audience of 215 people, many of whom I had never met.

The rest of the day didn't involve anyone fanning me with leaves or feeding me grapes. In full hair and makeup, I spent my last hours as a single woman on the toilet trying to push out anything and everything that would hold me back from being the most exquisite bride anyone had ever seen. Even a rabbit pebble would do. I couldn't disrespect my guests who'd all gifted me checks in multiples of eighteen dollars (in Judaism, eighteen is a number that represents luck) by showing up with a belly that gave the trumpet silhouette of my dress more of a French horn vibe.

My inability to remember a play-by-play of the entire morning of my wedding three years later inspires a tremendous amount of guilt. I should have been walking on goddamn sunshine all day, pausing every so often to pull out my purple fuzzy journal to document everything I saw, thought, and felt. Instead, I fretted over whether my bridesmaids thought my day-of gifts were lame (hand-painted wooden boxes filled with beauty products, trinkets, and photos), whether Noah was even awake, and whether my digestive tract could pretty, pretty please not get all constipated and bloated on me the day I was expected to look like a frilly piece of tooth floss.

The wedding was everything a bubby could want for her granddaughter (also known as *aynickel*): it was complete with a *Lubavitch* officiant, gender-segregated seating, the *sheva brachot*, seven minutes locked in a room with my new husband while two rabbis waited outside to make sure we were actually consummating our marriage (we used the time to pick food out of our teeth), and a solid half hour of high-intensity *horah* circles. It was the same sanctuary where, fourteen years before, I recited my Bat Mitzvah *parsha* in front of all the cool kids in my class, including the ones who called me a slut. Getting married at an Orthodox synagogue is the least slutty thing I could have done, and I love that for me.

"Don't worry, you guys, just because I'm married, I'm still the weird freak you've always thought I was," I wanted to exclaim out loud to my guests once I got the mic to sing in the family band. In aiming to preserve my perceived mediocrity as a bride, the pressure wasn't on to perform for our guests and social media. If they knew to expect garbage, it wouldn't be so jarring when said trash did a twirl in her dress.

But was that me? Was it not the dress but my attempt to prove that I was a nice Jewish girl the real costume in question?

Despite regularly writing about weddings, I was the furthest thing you'd ever meet from your socially acceptable bride. A voice in my head—the same one that invaded my brain with lines from women's magazines—once told me that unless I slaved over every detail of the ceremony and reception, I didn't deserve to get married, I didn't actually care about my husband, and that I was a Bad Bride. *Even my Pinterest boards look like shit*, I used to think to myself while browsing random subreddits for pitch ideas for my regular wedding contributions to *Vogue*. My editors were out of their minds for giving me a platform to write about and report on a topic I completely failed at in real life. If I couldn't get my shit together for my own wedding, clearly I was in no position to help my millions of readers do the same.

I felt lonely in not sharing in the sentiments of other prospective brides who fretted over flowers and panicked over place cards. In my eyes, it lent them an air of control and grace. They spoke in code laced with words like votives and boutonnieres and tulle, and made demands in ways I was always afraid of emulating—whether I was looking for a dress that fit, negotiating my salary, or asking a drunken stranger to stop touching my lower back. I didn't even think about my wedding enough, according to the general discourse surrounding weddings. The day barely crossed my mind until friends bombarded me with questions about how I felt or where I was in the elusive wedding schedule. When in doubt, "a few days away from my *mikvah* appointment" was an answer that satisfied most.

The whole thing might have felt in line with my truth had we started with a dress that actually fit, that allowed me to sit up straight, and didn't feature straps that cut into my shoulders like knives. We shame prospective brides for being vain, for wanting to look perfect. But it pays to feel perfect, too. It didn't matter that I totally screwed up the rules—during a belated fact-check for one of my *Vogue* articles, I learned my dress should have, in fact, been backless with a more minimal aesthetic. But abiding by that rule wouldn't have given me the perfect wedding, nor would offering my bridesmaids noncheesy gifts or performing a more YouTube-viral-worthy mosh pit (although that part was a redeeming quality). The only thing that would have made my wedding a success was if I chose not to have one altogether. In trying so hard to avoid being That Bride who demands something as basic as a dress that doesn't rearrange her organs, I relinquished my one opportunity to start life as a married woman who advocates for herself, who asks for what she wants and settles for nothing less.

Sure, I may not know my tulle from my tweed. But I got to say I spent forty-five minutes alone in the bridal room doing *BuzzFeed* quizzes while eating French fries, and it was the happiest I had felt in months. I left the bridal room with the very important knowledge that I should think about going blonde and moving to France, according to my responses. I might not have had my magazines to guide me through the day like they were Bluetooth earpieces walking me through all the steps, down the aisle. But I cherished those forty-five minutes as my opportunity to emotionally unbutton those six thousand clasps so I could finally take a full inhale and exhale. I had the rest of my life to hold my breath like the nice Jewish girl I am.

Chapter 12

PUSSY POWER

I kissed my three sweet boys good-bye before heading to the airport. Hunter, a four-year-old tabby with the disposition of a calloused war veteran, curled his tail into a question mark when I rubbed his arched lower back. Bucky, an eight-month-old rescue kitten and my birthday present from Noah, stretched his cinnamon roll–shaped body into an outstretched Y when I gave him a big squeeze. I snapped a picture in case I ran out of things to talk about at my lavish dinners with industry people I barely knew. I planted Noah's thin, soft lips with a long, closed-mouth kiss. Had I done anything more, I would have been tempted to reschedule my Uber.

Leaving Noah for days at a time used to trigger full-blown bulimia episodes. What kind of porn was he watching? Were the girls prettier than me? He better flush the used Kleenex so the cats don't get to them.

"We'll be waiting right here on this Craigslist couch for you when you get back," he said.

I shut the door and proceeded to spend the entire Uber ride doing what I do best: stalking Noah's ex-girlfriends on social media even though we had been married for over a year by that point, and looking up videos of cats because the love I had for my own was so much to sit with I had to outsource some of that obsession. I liken it to when your infatuation for someone feels so overwhelming you need to offload some of that energy into going on a date with someone else so you can loosen your grip on the first one. By doing that, I end up sabotaging whatever I had with said primary object of my obsession, but at least he never needs to learn just how batshit-level invested I really am. Luckily, my cats don't have any sort of batshit detector that I know of—but being so in love, so unchill, and so devoted was not an emotion I had yet learned to lean into.

Twenty-minute Uber rides always went by in a heartbeat when I had cats to look at, so my driver had to subtly kick me out of his Toyota. Judging by his exasperated tone, it seemed like multiple times. When I went through security, TSA nearly flagged me for carrying an entire zoo's worth of cat hair on my clothes.

"I carry my babies with me everywhere I go," I said without a strand of sarcasm to the burly woman carrying a baton. She was just doing her job. Or maybe she just wanted an excuse to talk to me. I went through every possible scenario in my head, and all of them involved her potentially wanting to fuck me. It was a rare moment of egomania that I promised myself I'd mentally reference in moments of sudden and unexplainable self-hatred when I landed in Los Angeles, like the hatred I experience when I don't even let myself mentally travel to a place where I love someone and they love me back in equal measure. It's dangerous to tempt myself with such a concept in case I get too addicted to it.

My schedule was filled with workshops, so I should have slept on the plane if I wanted to stay awake, but Gina—my longtime partner in all things freelance journalism—regaled me with gossip the entire flight that fed my soul like a breaking-the-fast dinner on Yom Kippur. I flipped through photos of my cinnamon roll of a pet and despite being forty thousand feet above sea level, instantly felt tethered to the ground back on that Craigslist couch with him and my two other boys.

Upon landing, Gina and I grabbed an obligatory over-priced airport Starbucks latte so we could fake our way into looking and acting like functional human beings. With my free hand, I hung my weekend bag over my shoulders and walked toward the valet pickup, our first and last names displayed embarrassingly prominently on whiteboards. Taking cues from celebrities photographed in airports (because egomania), I held my head high yet made eye contact with no one as I strode down my proverbial catwalk. This was LAX, after all. I wasn't about to "green light" the whole airport and look approachable. It was important to look like I had been there before, even though every cell in my body was on fire with shame at how sweaty I got on the plane despite everyone else wrapping themselves in blankets cozier than the gestational sac they once called home.

Our driver handed us mini water bottles with Ritz-Carlton logos slapped on. I was thankful for them not only so I could cool off and stop imprinting an inkblot of sweat in the shape of my own ass on his leather seats but also so one day I'd have a place to store vodka when I was carrying around a small purse and a standard 591-milliliter bottle just wouldn't do. A mousy receptionist showed me to my villa, reminding me why the whole covered-in-cat-hair and smelling like an actual litterbox wasn't the aesthetic I wanted to be remembered by. I couldn't compete with the veritable models and celebrities parading around the Ritz-Carlton courtyard (their thigh gaps were personal affronts), so I did what any peasant would do. I curled up on the bed's bajillion thread-count sheets on which thousands of other people got messy blowjobs and removed every piece of clothing that had compromised my circulation on the flight and that caused me to ooze perspiration at the sight of anyone marginally hotter than me. The endeavor devolved into a solo game of strip poker. The hair on my skin stood tall as I strode past my soft body in the mirror. Starbucks bloat had to be a real thing. There was no way I looked like that.

Before I got a chance to become one with the mattress, Noah's name appeared on my screen. He was great about

FaceTiming me whenever I landed, and I always answered after half a ring. I didn't know how to play it cool and wait three rings. I needed to hear his voice, hear him acknowledge me. Right. The fuck. Away.

"Hi, Sweetie. How was your flight? You get in okay?" he said.

"All is good. Nothing to really report besides the confirmation that I'm the grossest and fattest person in this area code," I said, fully aware my therapist would telepathically slap me across the face for that one. I knew he was pitching a story to a major men's magazine about my eating disorder and how to navigate it from the perspective of a spouse or partner, so I made sure to give him lots of fodder for his editor. Anything for journalism.

"Sweetie, you're not fat," he said. "I don't know how many times I have to tell you," he said. He could have been saying, "You're not the color blue." That's how little his words of confirmation soaked in.

"If I'm not fat, explain why every single one of my crevices is leaking like a faucet and I'm not even horny," I said.

"Okay, enough, there's something we need to talk about. Listen to me and cut it out with the anxiety for a sec," he said.

"I'm listening," I replied, fully aware that I could not and would not turn my anxiety off like a light switch just because he said so. But I appreciated his faith in me.

"We have to put him down," he said. He looked pixelated on my tiny screen.

Excuse me, what?

"This can't be about Bucky. No," I said, as if my defiance definitively had any bearing on biology.

Noah's tears meant he wasn't kidding. He only cried when he spoke about his grandfather, his Papa. I lifted the top sheet above my shoulders, my nudity suddenly in poor taste given the content of the announcement. Before I left for the airport, Bucky was the feline embodiment of the cat emoji with hearts for eyes. He was so happy it didn't seem real. We had assumed his decreased appetite and reduced energy was a growth plateau or a response to the summer heat. He'd be back to normal if we just continued to rub his tummy, let him lick our entire faces like a trip to the spa for a microdermabrasion session, and present him with horrifying spiders to murder with his nails and teeth.

Within five minutes of the appointment, the vet diagnosed him with terminal leukemia, Noah continued. I almost wished we had Bucky sign a Do Not Resuscitate sometime earlier in his kittenhood so I wouldn't have to make this decision on my own, without his consent, against his strong, powerful will. There had to be life behind those big kitten hearts for eyes.

Noah could sense the unease in my voice as I struggled to recall what I learned in college biomedical ethics, so he chimed in. Surely, the rules did not apply here, but I needed something, anything to guide me through a decision I felt I had no business making.

"We need to put him down today. He's suffering, Marissa. Do you really want to do this to him?" he said.

His stubbly face looked even more pixelated through my glassy tears. Still naked under the covers with the vet standing right there, I was afraid to move in case it instigated a Butterfly Effect and hurt my fragile little furball. But Noah's decision was all I needed to cement my own. Instead, I wanted them to wait forty-eight hours for me until I got home from my trip so I could kiss my Bucky one last time. I hadn't known a love like that since my mom took me to see *Spice World* at the Cavendish Mall twenty years before. The chances of finding love like that again were slim.

* * *

The morning of Mother's Day 2018 was like any other Mother's Day—sons in their mid-thirties rushed to the flower store for last-minute bouquets and the sun gleamed over outdoor brunch tables swarming with busy and hungry families. The only thing that was off was—surprise, surprise—me.

My knockoff Juicy Couture velour sweatpants stuck to my skin as I peeled myself off the couch. I got up quietly and gently so as not to shift Bucky's fragile little body. Save for his heaving ribcage and fluttering whiskers, he laid there motionless for nearly twelve hours straight. Having just sat through a cross-continental flight, my legs were already halfway toward developing deep vein thrombosis, so a five-pound cat wouldn't do much more in the way of harm, I thought. I took my phone out of my fake Juicy Couture sweatpants pocket and proceeded to take closeup shots of

Bucky's face, and videos of his chest heaving up and down with the cadence of his shallow breaths. In five years, I thought, I'd need concrete evidence that he waited those forty-eight hours—just for me. But that wasn't enough.

I tucked Bucky into my cardigan as I walked through the threshold of the vet's office. Six minutes later, we were ushered into an empty examination room that reeked of animal remains and cyanide. I signed a few waivers without reading them and moved to the back of the room to make way for the vet technicians and all their various gear. Noah and I clutched each other by the waist as they poked and prodded at our little Bucky. I pulled away from Noah as our shared body heat became too much to handle on top of the grief. Bucky's small incision of a mouth fell agape, and that's when the camera came back out. In the six months I knew him, I barely had a chance to comprehend that he was mine, that he was alive, he existed. Photos of his motionless body were the only way I could reasonably make sense of his death—this time on my own terms without the forty-eight-hour countdown.

* * *

The apartment felt dark and quiet when I returned empty-handed. For days, Hunter cried while looking for his adoptive brother as he moved from room to room. Friends and family stopped by with Boustan takeout and Hallmark cards, but ultimately Noah was the only other person who could understand my pain. By virtue of that, he was also a walking reminder of the pain I couldn't rid myself of.

Our home was emptier yet somehow felt smaller. Too small, even. The only solution was to dilute the pain with more space, more floors, a bigger kitchen, marble tiles, a yard, a walk-in closet, three bedrooms, and a nursery. We weren't ready for kids, but we would be after the Trump administration, we told family and friends whenever they asked. We couldn't just say, "Oh, we're trying next month!" because then they would have imagined him raw dogging me and I'd rather my parents think of me as celibate than in some compromising position. We'd fill those rooms up with babies no problem, we said. We'd pop out enough kids for a *minyan*, just watch, we said. So a home in suburban *Notre-Dame-de-Grâce* is precisely what we bought.

Within an hour of posting the ad for our current apartment, we had already gotten five requests for a visitation. Normally, I would have needed to devise some arbitrary strategy to determine who gets priority, but this was a no-brainer: Brian, a friend I hadn't spoken to in several years, was having a bad day and really needed a win. The only thing that would possibly remedy his own personal hell, he said, would be my first-floor bright apartment that happened to be down the street from his best friend.

"What kind of personal hell are we talking here, bud?" I typed back.

"My cat is going to die any day now and I just can't take it," he said. Having watched him open a beer bottle with his nipple at one of my famous barbecues in 2012, we were way past formalities, so the bluntness of his comment after a decade of not talking felt like more of a continuation of a previous conversation than an entirely new one.

"That's heartbreaking. I'm so sorry," I said. "I know all about that if you want to talk. And also, the apartment is yours if you want it."

"That's really kind of you," he said. "I needed that today. By the way, the appointment is tomorrow at 1:30."

It was unseasonably cool for a Montreal spring afternoon, so I threw on a jacket and walked the eight blocks to the Animal Health Clinic in front of Girouard Park. I noticed an emptiness to my hands. The last time I had stepped through the clinic's threshold, a wailing kitten was enduring one seizure after another in my arms.

It didn't take long before I spotted Brian. His slick, bald head glowed under the waiting room's fluorescent lighting. Beside him was a thin and elegant orange cat. Suai—meaning "beauty" in Thai—looked at me inquisitively. I could tell she was smart. She had a degenerative disease that was causing her lots of pain, but it didn't compromise her motility or curiosity. She was just tired in her little cage, yet retained a sort of wisdom that only comes with having seen some shit.

Without saying a word, I draped an arm around Brian's broad shoulder, careful not to touch him in a way that would upset his wife who was out of town. It was slouched over as he rested his forehead in his hands.

"I'm here. I'm here," I said quietly, while gingerly patting his shoulder with one hand. I didn't want my sudden movements or loud gestures to inflict any more pain on Suai. Like a Butterfly Effect.

"Thanks for coming. It means a lot. I knew you would," he said.

"Of course," I said. "I can't imagine going through something like this alone. I don't know what I would have done if Noah wasn't there throughout this whole process with me."

"Before we go in, there's one thing you should know," he said.

"What's up?" I asked.

"Suai does not like other women. She's very protective of me and is just generally bitchy to girls."

"I'm not worried," I said, digging up that sense of egomania I discovered at LAX that I stowed away for safe-keeping in moments of sudden and unexplainable self-hatred.

After brief silence, Brian got called into the empty animal remains- and cyanide-smelling examination room.

"I'll just have you pop her down right there, sir," said the baby-faced gray-haired vet, fastening on his various doctorly devices. Judging by the way he was looking at me, he did not recall my nude moment of hysteria over FaceTime the year before when he delivered the news to me that my cat was better off dead. Or maybe he did, and he was just really good at adhering to biomedical ethics and pretending that exchange never happened. I felt betrayed. I thought we shared a moment together.

"So, what's next, doc?" Brian managed through trembling lips.

"I'm going to administer two needles," said the vet. "The first will act as a sedative. She'll get all comfy 'n cozy. The next will stop her heart. She won't feel a thing."

There was nothing left to say to each other, and only moments left until the vet technicians would strap Suai's skinny limbs down to the examination table. In this moment of limbo, the only thing that made sense to do was hold her and pet her and tell her it would be okay. She is so loved, I said. She will be so missed, I said.

It took her a moment to get comfortable in my arms, but she soon settled in as if they were two fleshy hammocks.

"Man, that's so weird. She never does that with anyone, let alone girls," Brian said.

"Told you I got this," I said, trying desperately to sound more comforting than cocky. The vet gave us a look suggesting he was ready to perform the procedure when we were. Suai spilled out of my arms like orange juice from a carton. The emptiness set in again. Or was it fullness? A satisfaction in knowing I was capable of loving? But to love who, and what? I had a husband, my default person to "love," but the answer wasn't so obvious when I felt an unprecedented need to protect this furry creature at all costs.

As one blonde-haired vet tech held Suai down by her limbs, the vet inserted his first round of needles. I knew how to say good-bye to pets. But it never got easier, as each one stung more than the last. That's the thing about grief. You never get better at it.

"I feel like sadness and loss just follows us wherever we go in this goddamn apartment," I said, throwing my jacket over the couch where Noah sat playing Red Dead Redemption when I got home from the vet.

"Well, good thing you're getting your way," he said.

"We agreed on this together," I said. "Don't act like it wasn't your choice to get a house, too. I saw the way you pranced around the open house all giddy at the idea of cooking all your intense four-hour stir-fry projects in that open-space kitchen."

I sat down closer to him so as not to come off as threatening. I was always adjusting my body language so as to make myself more palatable.

"But think about it," he said. "Once we get the house, there's really no option of ever trying to make the New York thing happen. We'd be stuck here forever."

It always came back to this. After my meeting with a senior editor at *Cosmo* four years earlier (prestarving myself, drinking way too much coffee, and fainting—fun!), I couldn't shake the idea that I needed to live there. I was always so embarrassed writing for all these top-tier American publications, unable to make it to New York–based magazine events because I lived a whole national border away. It was embarrassing to not fully understand the lingo. My identity as a Canadian outsider, a fraud who routinely covered American pop culture, politics, and products despite living in a totally different country, felt all too evocative of being ostracized and then reluctantly allowed to play *Blue's Clues* in the schoolyard. And without French as a main language in New York, I didn't feel like people were talking about me in secret code. *La Maudite juife*, *la saloppe*, I've heard under the buzz of my barely-noise-canceling headphones more times than I can count.

After dozens of dejected conversations with immigration lawyers and editors later, I finally relinquished that dream of moving to New York. It wasn't feasible. And so I made peace with the life I have now. The life I have here. With Noah and the cats.

* * *

My eyes had barely pried apart when I saw Noah perk up in bed at 10:00 a.m. on a Saturday in June 2020. This was early for us, but he often surprised me by having the coffee ready and waiting for me on our marble peninsula in the kitchen. So his early wake-up call wasn't particularly unusual.

The night before was like any other night. We were drinking our biweekly Moscow Mules on our back porch when I mentioned what I'd be making for dinner the coming weekend.

"We're learning this thing in my plant-based nutrition course where saturated fatty acids mimic the actions of lilopolysaccardies, which seep into the blood stream, fuck with your immune cells, and lead to inflammation, so I was thinking of baking the falafel this time instead of frying it," I said.

He looked at me blankly. I continued.

"Inflammation is one of the main risk factors for chronic disease, so it would mean a lot to me if we could take care of your nutrition. Together. We can start by limiting your—I mean *our*—intake of 'bad' fats."

I wasn't surprised when my suggestion was met with an eye roll and some variation of "You and your health bullshit, why can't anything taste good for once? Can you please stop inflicting your eating disorder on me?" He wasn't wrong. I always caught myself trying to nurture him through the lens of vitamins and minerals, when maybe I should have been doting on him like bubby did to me. With abundance, no restrictions, endless and boundless like the sky. Like I said, he was older and wiser and probably knew better, so I didn't argue. I was thankful for his guidance. My forever Sherpa up the hill.

"I prefer fried, otherwise there's no real point to falafel. But I'll give it a try," he said.

Not seven hours later, the bed rocked me awake far earlier than was normal for us on a weekend.

"Call my brother," he said. His voice was steady and firm. "Tell him I'm not feeling well."

"On it," I said without missing a heartbeat.

I dialed up his brother, who works in the medical field, and hurriedly explained Noah's symptoms.

"Probably just anxiety or digestive issues," his brother said. "For someone who's thirty-five years old, in perfect health, I wouldn't stress."

Noah slipped out of bed and staggered over to our bathroom. His body fell slack and he dropped to his knees. He then proceeded to heave into the toilet, and then nearly smashed his head collapsing to the ground. As if the conversation with his brother never even happened, I dialed 911 immediately.

"Hi, yes, my husband is currently on the floor and everything hurts can you please send someone immediately?" I said to the operator. Having felt like the girl who cried wolf all my life, I thought I did a poor job of proving to the woman that we needed serious help. Should I have been crying? Hyperventilating? Threatening my own life? What did it say about me—as a wife, as a person—that I couldn't remember the last time I felt so in control, and not inclined to take any of the aforementioned extreme measures? It was like my anxiety latched onto things that didn't matter, like how fat I looked on a given day or whether one of my hot queer editors liked me back, leaving my anxiety with no remaining energy to fixate on things that actually mattered, like whether my husband was able to overcome his full-body discomfort.

"Not to worry, ma'am. We are sending the paramedics to your location right away and they will be there shortly. I will stay with you on the phone until they arrive," she said. She had a sweet and calming voice, but no soft sound or sense of any kind could erode at the guilt sitting heavily between my throat and my lungs.

For twelve minutes, I held Noah's hand, but not too hard, so as not to hurt him more.

"They're on their way, Noah. Just keeping breathing, stay calm. We've got this," I said.

Agonizing bellows emanated from his thin lips. By now, a thin layer of glistening sweat coated his body like fresh paint on a park bench. I wasn't entirely confident that we had, indeed, "got[ten] this," but it seemed like the only appropriate thing to say in that moment.

"When are they coming?" he managed. "I'm in pain. So much pain."

A handful of minutes later, I let six burly men in blue and yellow vests through the front door. They carried duffel bags filled with equipment and a gurney covered in a red blanket.

"Let's go, buddy," one paramedic said, lifting Noah into his arms and onto the couch.

The sounds of six walkie-talkies all going off at once muffled any sound I tried to make, be it a question or a comment. Disposable medical device wrappers flung across the room as each paramedic got to work on a different part of his body. They fastened a tourniquet around his arm, stuck electrodes to his chest, and kept his head from tipping over to one side. As the only untouched part of his body, I ran my fingers through his thick head of dark hair. Gently, so as not to hurt him.

"Ma'am, we're going to need you to step aside. We have to administer some serious tests here, okay?"

There was no way to make sense of why this was happening to him, to me, to us, at a moment in time I wasn't even sure if we were an us. Two weeks earlier, I had asked for a separation. After two days of contemplating what my life might look like without him, how painful it might be to disentangle our lives, the deep shame I felt in leaving a marriage after three years at the young age of twenty-eight, I decided to try making it work one last time.

Noah was visibly distraught by now, his skin blending seamlessly with the gray cushions of our couch. But there was no way to pick up the pace more than the paramedics had already been doing—that is, unless I helped. To buy them more time, I agreed to help them lug their duffel bags into the ambulance as they affixed Noah to the gurney and wheeled him in. Neighbors poured out of their homes and onto the street like blood spilling out of a wound, *orange juice out of a carton*. I wondered if they judged me for not wearing any shoes or a bra. Of course they did—I was that grimy, unwashed woman-child on their street cosplaying as an adult because we, or maybe I, thought it "could be nice" to live in suburbia encircled by parks, green grass, and Volvos despite my aesthetic suggesting I belonged in a graffiti-splattered alley.

Because of the pandemic, I couldn't ride in the ambulance or stay with him in the hospital. All I could manage was a sheepish "I love you!" as the ambulance drove away leaving a stream of sirens in its wake. But did I mean it? Did I mean it two weeks earlier when I asked him for a separation because he couldn't shake the idea of New York any longer and wanted to apply to grad school and live in an apartment and travel more and have more fun and generally live a new and improved life? Did I mean it when, after two days of being separated, I asked him if we could give this whole marriage thing one last Hail Mary push because I couldn't fathom the idea of him living alone in his own undecorated bachelor pad, or have him move out in a pandemic when doing anything, anywhere is a massive risk? Did I mean it when I said I would rather stay put in Montreal near all my friends and family, but if I had to move to New York and be miserable, I would do it for him?

His first call after being admitted to the hospital intercepted my ability to draw any real conclusion about how I felt about him.

"Noah? Hello? Talk to me," I said into my cracked phone.

"Hi, yeah, I'm just waking up," he said groggily.

"Okay, but what the fuck just happened?"

"I'm alive, and that's all that matters, he said.

"No, seriously. Tell me what it was."

He described his medical emergency in painstaking detail: the pain, the fear, the shock. I gasped before pausing to cup my mouth in my hands because it felt like the appropriate response to news of this gravity.

"I'm not kidding," he said, filling the silence. "Scariest few hours of my life."

I felt guilty for feeling more relieved that he was alive, and less empathetic that he experienced that much pain. He continued to explain that they caught his issue early enough to prevent some serious damage. He would need another day or two to rest.

I thought about him a lot while he was in the hospital. But not in the way that a "normal wife" would, whatever that meant. I thought about him when I came back to myself in a way I could never do in his presence. My friends and I could speak loudly about eating ass without his eyerolls. I could eat cold vegetable soup straight out of the can while standing up. The hip-hop music blared from my tinny laptop speakers, a sound he couldn't stand, which was not his fault. I came on. I came back to myself. It was a brand of joy and freedom I never felt entitled to, and so I shut it down and forged ahead with the life I promised I would offer him when we stood in front of the arc of *torahs* three years earlier at my congregation. Now was especially not the time to address my needs. More than ever, this person needed me.

He relayed the brochure-amount of information his surgeon bombarded him with pre- and post-operation. I was impressed by how much information he retained despite having gone to some other dimension for a couple hours.

I perked up in my chair when he told me he happened to speak to a dietitian. With some educational background in nutrition and a whole life of thinking about food twenty-four/seven, I felt fully equipped to be there for him in this capacity, should he need to be cared for in that way, and hopefully contribute to his life more meaningfully than I was ever capable of doing in our last five years together. It was exciting even! A bonding experience!

"So? What did the dietitian say? What are their thoughts on baked falafel?" I asked, trying to lighten the mood.

"There's nothing to say. All the dietitian said was that I should keep doing what I'm doing," he said. I let his grocery list and daily meal schedule run through my mind. There were items on there and habits that bothered me that I couldn't dream of submitting my own body to (white bagels and margarine? I'd like to take that up with my internet eating disorder friends on Xanga . . .). At first I couldn't tell whether I was judging his diet through the lens of my eating disorder or if it was objectively unhealthy. But who was I trying to kid? The mere idea of knowing every bite he eats was pretty telling of an issue in and of itself.

I wasn't surprised he shut down the food conversation. I took that as a cue not to bring up the fact that I addressed his physical health the night before the incident, as if some magical force in me predicted it would happen. Now was not the time to be petty or put him in his place. But I refused to let my outrage—my feeling of utter invisibility—overtake my need to nurture him.

"I can't even imagine what you're feeling right now," I said. "What was going through your mind before they gave you the fentanyl?"

"Honestly? Pain and fear. Just pain and fear," he said. I waited for him to tell me he saw a bright light and decided life was too short to pick up and leave and start over in a new city, that he couldn't bear the thought of potentially dying and leaving me alone, that it pained him our last real conversation was about fried fucking falafel and he wished it never ended that way, so here's to a new beginning, let's start over, our life as we know it is enough for me. You, me, and the cats.

Those words, of course, never came.

"So . . . are you able to go back to work this week?" I asked, steering the conversation toward the technical so I wouldn't accidentally burden him with more questions about his nutrition plan.

"Certainly am."

I sat with that idea for a moment before he hung up to take a nap. Life would resume. It already had. And now what? And then what?

I left the conversation feeling unsatisfied, as if it didn't live up to the standard soap operas set when a loved one falls ill and everyone springs into hysterics. Sure, don't get me wrong, the whole thing was—and is—devastating and traumatic. But there had to be a reason why I felt so at ease holding down the fort in his absence.

After checking in on him via FaceTime and bringing him food and warm clothes for the next two days, he was ready to come home. I kept the profanities and the music down not only to protect his healing body but because my window to live as myself as I had initially known it and loved it had closed.

Standing under the hospital's veranda, he looked tired and worn, but not unlike the way he looked after, say, a full shift at work with a couple hours of overtime. When I got out of the car to help him in, he managed a one-handed hug that I wouldn't have been able to feel had I been wearing anything thicker than a cotton T-shirt in the June heat. I smelled the turquoise hoodie he was wearing to check if there was anything left of him.

The car ride was filled with dialogue you might share with a distant cousin you pick up at the airport who will be crashing on your futon for the next couple weeks.

"Great to have you back!" I said cheerfully.

"Yeah, it's good to be back. That was a close call," he said.

He took in his surroundings even though Decarie was a street we had driven on nearly six thousand times. I knew I couldn't ask him gory and private details about what the whole thing really felt like, like really, really felt like. But given how fragile he looked and felt—I used that as a litmus test and stuck to safe pleasantries instead.

"Did you sleep well in the hospital?" I asked.

"Yeah, it was pretty much all I did," he said.

I had nothing left to say or ask that he would feel comfortable with, so I rested my palm on top of his while we drove in silence.

I kept the house tidier than usual so he could feel at ease when he got home. After unpacking his hospital bag, I let him sleep, hoping his appetite would return by the time he woke up and dinner was ready. We were right on schedule for falafel night.

"This is really good," he said, biting into a chickpea patty that crumbled down his chin and into his four-day stubble. He was still woozy from his procedure, but he was still him at his core. Had he been totally out of it— and I mean out of it in the way I once cradled a male nurse's head right after a colonoscopy—then I would have let it slide. But he was all there, physically and mentally, saying, "Life is too short to wait around to chase my dreams. I've made so many excuses over the years as to why I shouldn't get a master's, why I shouldn't move to the States. And the more I think about it, the more I realize my time is now."

To buy myself some time before responding, I used a fork and knife to cut my falafel ball into eight imperceptible pieces, which I never do.

"That's really great," I said, opening my pursed lips just enough to sound audible. "I'll help you with your cover letters. I'll look into tuition and bursaries. Whatever you need, I'm here."

That part wasn't a lie. His ambition was inspiring to watch. But the same way it felt so good to honor my need for loud hip-hop music, cold leftovers, and filthy jokes, so too did I have to acknowledge how little intention I had of moving to any city that would have me just because it was "the cool thing to do" and I "needed to evolve." Promising to help move him closer to his goal felt like the only noble or socially acceptable way of pushing him farther from me so he'd leave organically, on his own terms, so it'd be mutual. And with his physical health complicating matters, optics were a thing I never wanted to consider, but kind of had to if I didn't want to become more of a social pariah than I already was.

The following day, I was actually excited to go to a barbecue at his parents' house. I was secretly hoping we could make amends. Life was too short, maybe they saw their own special bright light, maybe they would finally accept me as their daughter-in-law, flaws, quirks, messiness, and all. Instead, I watched silently as I picked at flakey salmon, and Noah, allergic to fish, dug into his cheese omelet. I wasn't looking for a Hero of the Year Award, but I was hoping my swift action in calling the paramedics was the icebreaker they needed to, at the very least, welcome me into their pack.

That conversation, of course, never came.

I knew from that moment it would be the last piece of flakey salmon I ever ate at their house.

That night, I couldn't contain the dull ache in my own abdomen, and I knew it wasn't the overcooked salmon. We were wordlessly performing our nightly bedtime routine of him browsing Reddit and me tweezing my bikini line while listening to a podcast. Even though I had plucked and prodded at my groin for the last forty-seven days straight, this one took on a new heaviness. It would be the last time I plucked and prodded as a fully married, not-separated woman.

"I can't do this anymore," I said in the dark. The same dark I used to hide my body from him. To hide from him and to hide from myself.

There were no dramatics, no sirens, no neighbors pouring out into the streets like wounds without a tourniquet. Just our two sullen faces illuminated by the dim light of our respective cell phones, facing a reality we had fought so hard both to fix and ignore. The dark made the declaration feel as impersonal as a green text sent to an iPhone, or a voice mail you check nine days later when the message doesn't matter anymore and it's just too late.

"If this is what you want, I don't have the energy to fight anymore," he said. I waited for him to tell me he saw a bright light and decided life was too short, that he needed me, he would do anything, let's have a fresh start. Instead, we both slumped over to our respective sides of the bed and whimpered softly into our pillows.

"When I told you we were going to get through this together, I meant it with every bit of me," I said after our obligatory two minutes of repressed tearing and nothing else. "I'm going to be here for you in whatever way you need me to be. I'll take you wherever you need to go, I'll make sure you have food, I'll listen to you vent. Just because I don't think we can make each other happy in the long-term, it doesn't mean my care for you ends here."

I rubbed his shoulders out of a genuine sense of tenderness, ignoring the fact this would be the last time I would be "allowed" to interact with him in that way if I sought a legally binding separation. It made me think of all the times I got dumped by guys in high school with the qualifier that they still cared about me and thought I was great, but it was just not working out. It turns out those gangly teens might have been telling the truth all along. Forget shades of gray—emotions occupy every color of the spectrum. Some colors are just a little prettier than others.

* * *

I could have advocated for myself in the cold and damp camp cabin ten years earlier, or on the examination table at the gynecologist's office, or when my high school English teacher told me to stop bragging when I notified her I won a national poetry competition that she told me to enter. But in truth, there would never be a right time to ask for what I wanted and steer clear of what I don't. And so the time would always be now. I don't regret a single moment of marriage. I saw the world, I ignored the allergist's recommendation to never go near cats again lest I wish to completely destroy my immune system (and as a result parented a total of four cats I will have tattooed on me by the time this book is published), and through the gaps that grew between Noah and I, I saw them exist within myself. A gap isn't a flaw. It's room to grow. I might not grow like a houseplant with a heart when you move me abroad or give me a shiny new degree. I might not be great with change and the unknown. But what I do have is a fascination with nurturing what already exists inside me and around me instead of searching for something new.

I'm still trying this revelation on for size—swiveling it around my tongue like Listerine—hoping to one day extend that same patience toward the way I feel about my being and my body, the thing that has quite literally never left my side but that I continue to beat and maim and torture. I might thrive elsewhere one day, but my place is right here, right now. Right here in my messy home office where I will stay for eternity because two cats are currently sleeping on me and it would be a federal crime to wake them up. Right here with the same friends I've known for years—who've drawn genitalia all over the margins of my notebook or watched me play matchmaker with Barbie and Ken, and newer friends I've met as we clumsily navigated this whole Real Life thing together. Right here in the neighborhood not far from where I had my first kiss in the Cavendish Mall pirate ship or took too big of a hit on a battered couch from the free stuff section on Craigslist. About a fifteen-minute walk from coffee shops where I've made life-altering decisions over a sickeningly sweet cup of caffeine and Splenda. My life might be a big question mark, but I choose to see it as the shape of my cat's tail when she's happy. The signs are always right there in front of you.

Chapter 13

THE MORNING AFTER

You thought this was a book about struggling with
my identity all my life, leaving a broken marriage,
listening to a few self-help podcasts, and immediately getting my shit together? You flatter me!

I thought I'd come out of my divorce a wise old woman
with luscious gray hair and wrinkles around my eyes from
being so goddamn pensive and insightful all the time.
Instead, I was back to square one. I was googling shit my
sixteen-year-old self would know the answer to, like "Are
heels too much for a first date??" and "How does one pro-
cure enough confidence to order anything but a salad??"

For so long, my identity was "wife." And that was a comfortable space in which to exist. Every woman knows how to perform the role of wife—it's been drilled into our heads since the days of playing House in kindergarten when we wished on rogue eyelashes and folded Lay's chips that our crushes would agree to be our playtime husbands and we could raise dolls and stuffed bears but never once make eye contact. As the role of the wife, even my five-year-old self knew I had to perform a lot of doting, nurturing, tending, maybe a little nagging if I was feeling extra. But nowhere does the royal They teach us how to be divorced.

Once Noah packed his final suitcase, I looked around the barer lower duplex and felt at a loss of identity. I was no longer a wife. I wasn't quite single. I wasn't yet divorced. How was I supposed to navigate this liminal space? I had no magazine, no Sherpa up the hill advising me on how to move on and when it would be okay to do so. I had no Designated Cool Older Female to tell me she understood what I was going through and that it's okay to feel lost, alone, and confused. No one I knew my age was leaving their marriages—it was all my parents' friends who'd been together for thirty years.

Without some sort of authority figure's permission to feel pain, I numbed myself out. My pain wasn't valid because I didn't have three kids and a lifetime of family vacations behind us. I wasn't the perfect divorcee you could understand or relate to. I wasn't the divorced protagonist you see in romantic comedies where you leave the theater feeling so darn good about everything because the divorcee found herself within like thirty seconds of signing the papers and then opened a gluten-free bakery two scenes later.

While we're talking bakeries, when I left my marriage, I was the shitty lower part of the muffin because some asshole just ate the top half. I didn't become some fancy sweet dessert behind a glass case that's hard to pronounce like *croquembouche*. Muffin garbage, I was. Day old, too. And I came with more baggage than Noah's literal suitcase.

In an informal call with my divorce lawyer, I asked when it would be okay to start dating once we got separated.

"Technically you could start this second, but I would wait around six months," she said.

"Oh, why's that?" I asked.

"Well, you probably have lots of healing to do," she replied.

HA! Healing is for bitches, I thought, but didn't say out loud. It was cute that she had enough faith in me to take the emotionally healthy route. But why heal when you could smoke a joint at 11:00 a.m. every morning praying some fucking loser with a backward baseball hat will text me a meme because the pain of being ignored is unbearable to do sober? Why heal when you can get hyper-obsessed with curating the perfect Instagram feed so future suitors know who they're fucking with? Why spend time healing when the process of addressing and reflecting on pain is often more painful than the pain itself?

Something they don't teach you in grade school is that when you enter a relationship expecting the other person to fulfill a specific role in your life, it's bound to fail. Noah was so many things to me, chief among them my source of reassurance. *You're not fat. You're not dumb. You're a great cook. You're funny.* I assigned so much meaning to his words that I didn't even bother to interrogate whether I believed those things about myself. He was older and smarter, so naturally, his opinion of me prevailed. Without him, I had no echo chamber to remind me of all these things I'm supposed to think of myself in the first place.

I wish I could tell you I was a boss ass bitch about the whole thing—that growing apart in my marriage allowed me to rely on myself for validation and support outside of it. But your brain on divorce does this really cool thing where it gets obsessed with newness. It analyzes every single interaction with new potential dates; it inspires you to fix-ate on your flaws and vow to make them disappear in order to make yourself more palatable to this New Person. It's a big jump to go from texting a New Person here and there "Thinking of u [It emoji of the moment]," coming straight from a previous daily life of "Please stop farting so loud you're startling the cats."

I knew comfort. I knew routine. I knew Noah was going to buy lots of hummus and coffee creamer on his grocery runs, and that he'd wear his slip-on loafers to take out the recycling. I was even able to predict his answers to my questions before I asked them. So when a New Person interacted with me in a way that felt very off-script compared to the life I thought I'd lead when I stood in front of 215 of our closest friends announcing our eternal pact, the googling and the panicking began almost immediately. But something else happened that nothing could have prepared me for (we'll get to what that was later, I just felt like sounding dramatic).

The first exchange went something like this:

Him: You have the least decorated bedroom I've ever seen.

Me: Excuse me?

Writes down our future kids' names

When I post Instagram Stories, I don't actually think random people will look at them. So when a random person replies to something, I immediately feel turned on by how creepy, intrusive, and stalkerish it feels. I assumed that because I rarely looked at strangers' Stories, no one would look at mine. Like, there is literally nothing to see here unless you're interested in videos of my cats fellating each other and a few camcorder dad-quality videos of bubby responding to a question about how her day went.

He was a guy I had known for years through friends, but we never exchanged more than a few words besides me trying to set him up with a friend, and him pointing out that he saw me walking on Monkland. He was a stranger for all intents and purposes. He replied to one of my stories where I was testing out jeans for a *USA Today*'s Reviewed article (no, you can't have my job, yes, it is the only redeeming aspect of my life at any given moment), and I wanted my editor to see how balls-deep into the assignment I was. So, I modeled some products on Instagram before uploading them to the content management system the next day. Naturally, my editor responded with a flame emoji. Unnaturally, this person I had known for years but never really spoke to made like a summer backyard activity and slipped 'n slid into the ol' direct messages.

I had always thought of Alessio as a human hangnail—something that's kind of annoying to have around, but bearable if you ignore it. He was by no means the life of the party. He was something blurred in the background of a Monet painting. A blurred hangnail in a Monet painting. There it is. I wasn't even following him back, so his message first went straight to my Other inbox where the peasants live. I loved the power dynamic right off the bat. He was a nobody. Until he wasn't.

"It's no excuse that you just moved in. You gotta decorate," he continued after my feeble excuse for posing in front of the bare background that was my bedroom.

"When I walk into HomeGoods I just get overwhelmed and want everything, so I end up choosing nothing," I said.

"I'm the same way, but you just gotta make a decision and stick to it," he said.

I loved how bossy he was. How much he cared about such a specific, minute aspect of my life. I latched onto his attention for dear life like I used to do when I was invited to rock climbing birthday parties in grade three and kind of just stood there midwall clinging onto a single rock because any movement or deviation would send me tumbling ass-first.

It just so happened that I had been addictively playing a game called Home Design several hours a day where you enter room décor challenges and vote on the best looks. I was so into it that I spent real money on it just to get more points. I woke myself up in the middle of the night to check my scores. Home décor became such a profound interest of mine that for a fleeting second, my sister and I decided to open a real estate agency and call it Golden House. I needed someone to care about my interests because on some level, it compensated for all the hours I've spent on a boy's couch pretending to like football.

Like a question mark on my cat's happy tail, I saw the signs in him everywhere. He cared about home décor. We had the same favorite ice cream flavor (pistachio). We both had the same star sign (Scorpio). We grew up a couple blocks from each other (in *Côte-Saint-Luc*). Without knowing anything more than our surface-level similarities, I decided I was going to do anything it took to get him to want to be my boyfriend. But given my recent separation from Noah, I had no intention of actually dating him.

After a few weeks of hanging out, I made the very grave mistake of telling him I didn't want to see anyone else.

"But, like, not like to lock you down or anything. I'm just like *sooo* busy and too much of a scatterbrain to handle seeing multiple guys at once, so like you're totally free to do whatever you want but like, I'll be here I guess, sort of!" I justified over text.

"It took you this long to figure out I'm better than everyone else?" he said. The cockiness was so jarring and uncalled for that I found it irresistibly hot. And if he actually cared about being "better than everyone else," he must have had some (fore)skin in the game.

"Well, like, what do you think of what I just said?" I replied to his cryptic yet hope-inspiring comment.

"I have a few thoughts. We'll talk about it later," he said.

That night, he was supposed to meet me outside Jenna's house when I was done having salad and organic fruit and drinking wine with her and her husband. It was rare to feel so in the moment, so present with my friends. This person occupied so much of my brain space that I often forgot where I was when I got a text from him. Mid-bite of tomato, I looked down at my phone and noticed several texts and missed calls from Alessio.

"I've been waiting for fifteen minutes and I'm hungry so I'm going home," one of the messages read.

Fuck. I forgot that I had turned his text notifications to Do Not Disturb. Weird choice, but here's why: when I got a text from him, it was like time stopped. It was what I imagine cocaine feels like. It was starting to get exhausting, going from an endorphin surge to a rapid crash so frequently. I imagined it's what happens in diabetics when an insulin surge leads to an energy crash. I was drowning in the waves. It wasn't a feeling that was particularly conducive to sanity, productivity, or independence.

He left. After some coercing to come back downstairs and talk to me, he obliged. I felt honored that, midprotein shake and basketball game, he gave me a morsel of his time.

Before going into the lobby of his building, I used a strand of hair to get a piece of organic arugula out of my teeth. I then did the very presumptuous thing of dialing his apartment number on the keypad in the lobby so I could go up to his unit. When he said we can talk for a few minutes outside, I assumed he meant on his balcony covered in real plants and actual patio furniture. The balcony we ate home-made tofu curry on and got yelled at by noise-sensitive neighbors on. I didn't realize he meant literally outside, away from his actual living space.

He came downstairs wearing basketball shorts that revealed a considerable amount of his upper ass cheek. His blue and gray striped shirt and thongs—like the stuff for your butt but the toe version—suggested he cared very little about impressing me. Getting him to talk to me felt like I was a belayer anchoring down a rock climber who just wanted to get as far away from the ground as possible. Clearly this whole rock climbing thing never has and never will work out for me, so I am unavailable to attend your third-grader's birthday party.

"So, what'd you want to talk about?" he said, either because he was playing dumb or actually was not a particularly intelligent person.

I set my bike down against a big rock and we both sat on the other side of it, not touching.

"I don't know, that thing. You said you had some thoughts," I said.

After analyzing his texts, my friends said I had nothing to worry about, so I didn't worry (funny how I'll let some bitch named Ashley in a cropped tie-dye hoodie with a drinking problem dictate my life, but not a boy, no siree Bob).

I was mostly anxious to see him because I wanted to force an answer out of him. What he thought about that statement. What he thought about the way I asked for what I wanted instead of letting him guide the dynamic. The whole idea of a "Let's talk later" situation was anxiety inducing enough. I didn't want to make the mistake of predicting his emotions or following a script like I waited for Noah to do when he got out of the hospital. Predicting and anticipating led to inevitable disappointment, and I was tired, so tired, of letting guys wearing backward baseball caps decide how I live, think, and feel.

"I just think you're way more invested in this than I am," he said with folded arms. "Like you want to see me way more than I want to see you, you rely on me for a lot of reassurance, you just got out of a marriage. That shit's heavy." Despite apologizing numerous times for how "bad" he was at talking about serious things, I thought he did a stellar job of communicating his boundaries. Boundaries have never been my strong suit. In case you couldn't tell, I'm the type to let you shit in front of me on the first date.

Fat, bulbous tears streamed down his cheeks as he spoke. He was many things, this person. Funny, generous, confident. The crying type was not one of them.

"Don't put words in my mouth," I said. "I don't want to get involved with you at all. In fact, I think you'd make a terrible boyfriend, I find you annoying, you're not that smart, and you have some really backward views. I don't even want you. I want you to want me." I was now turning away so I wouldn't cry, too.

"God, I'm cool," he said.

We went back and forth for a little while, where I argued that it was totally his fault that I caught feelings, or whatever they were, because he sent me good morning texts. GOOD MORNING texts. There are people out there who surprise their partners with morning head and full continental breakfasts, and I was out here circling our initials in hearts because he pressed a couple buttons on his phone while clocking into work.

"I don't know what I need right now, but I do know you deserve better," he said.

"Don't say that! I can be whatever you want me to be! Just say it! Name it! I'll do it! I'll be it!" It was single-handedly the most pathetic sentence to ever be uttered this side of *Côte-Saint-Luc*. After all, living in this liminal space between married, single, and divorced was the perfect time to reinvent myself. He could have suggested I become a battered dog and I would have found a way to make it happen.

"Don't change for me or for anyone," he said.

By this point, I was sobbing into his chest while tears from his eyes poured down the back of my shirt. For two kids who had been Twitter DMing for just a little over six weeks, it sure was an intimate moment incongruous with our given situation.

I let my emotions get chaotic because I decided they weren't my problem anymore. They were things outside of me with their own central nervous systems. If I relinquished accountability for my emotions, I didn't have to feel so guilty for the way they were manifesting themselves in my everyday life. For the way they veered off script. Here I was, twenty-eight years old, barely divorced, and crying in the middle of the road at 11:00 p.m. because this guy would rather play video games and watch sports than text me back or—gasp—take me on a date. Meanwhile, my other fish to fry were so big they barely fit in the pan: I left my husband, he was recovering from a near-death experience, I had a book to write, books to read, a job writing about fashion and beauty and home décor for *USA Today*, cats to look after, a home to preserve, friendships to nourish, and a family to love. Had I been some semblance of a normal person, I would have been too preoccupied fulfilling all of those other essential roles in my life to give a shit about what this veritable fuckboy had to say about me. It was as if I had forgotten everything I had learned to hone in marriage, like strong communication, trust, and compassion. Instead, I showed up to the world, walked into its lobby, and dialed its apartment number as one of those broken, ragged dolls that watch you while you sleep, looking for permission from someone, anyone, to feel like Barbie.

I wiped my boogers on a leaf I found on the ground and hopped back on my bike. "Thank you," I said to Alessio. "That is all the information I need to know."

"Well, what information? I didn't give you an answer," he said.

"No answer is always an answer," I said, proud of myself for quoting something he'd probably never heard of even though it was as basic and ubiquitous as "live, laugh, love."

I spent the next few days borderline impressed with myself for managing to get my heart broken in two places: one, for trying and failing to make my marriage work, and two, for trying and failing to get a boy to be obsessed with me as a way to heal heartbreak number one. Instead of doing this whole healing thing you self-help hashtag influencer life coaches talk about, I tried to fit five years' worth of emotions and situations into my six-week stint with the New Person. It would be my do-over, proof to myself I just needed to fling myself into the same situations over and over again until I was able to flawlessly perform the choreographed dance of modern romance like a Tik Tok eight count we teach ourselves to have things in common with people we find prettier or more successful than we are. It wasn't okay for part of my dance to include a slip and fall. What would the audience think of me? What if my exes spread lies about me? What if they said mean things about me behind my back, and worst of all, that those things would be true?

I'd like to rephrase an old adage that has historically held me back: they say in order for anyone to love you, you first need to love yourself. That is a massive undertaking! We can't reasonably go from wanting to literally hurl ourselves off a building one day to watching ourselves masturbate in the mirror the next. Self-love will always be a work-in-progress. But want to know the best part? We don't even need to wait until we reach this nebulous self-love thing to be worthy of it. Simply existing in our own bodies while aiming to lead rich and rewarding lives is enough. Not every type of love we seek—whether it be with another person or ourselves—needs to be so all-encompassing we forget what and who we are at the drop of a text. Love can be this gentle blanket of comfort or a nearly imperceptible pang of excitement. The less I look for the perfect type of magazine-approved love, the more I'm surprised by what I discover along the way, and that maybe, just maybe, I never even needed it to begin with.

ACKNOWLEDGMENTS

Thank you to my incredible friends, family and colleagues for helping me bring this book to life. Thanks to my rock star literary agents Carrie Howland from Howland Literary and Kathleen Schmidt and Andrea Barzvi from Empire Literary for championing the book from the very beginning. Thanks to my incredible editors at Skyhorse Publishing, Caroline Russomanno and Rebecca Shoenthal, for truly "getting it." Thanks to some of the most brilliant industry people I've had the privilege of working with and learning from over the years: Tim Herrera, Hanna Howard, Sade Strehlke, Mireille Silcoff, Basem Boshra, Jessie Van Amburg, Samantha Matt, Amanda Tarlton, Courtney Campbell, Kevin Gray, John Dioso, Lauren del Turco, Kristine Thomason and so many more. Shout out to my amazing friends who've brainstormed ideas for this book with me, provided honest feedback, and served as sources of unparalleled content: Michelle Miller (her name will be repeated shortly), Miranda Tuwaig, Michelle Azimov, Rachel Rappaport, Yarden Holzer, Anna Rosenfield, Elizabeth Tomaras, Ashley Joseph, Marlee Kostiner, Michael Miller, Daniel Zimmermann, Rachel Sheiner, Andrew Brownstein, Hayes Nulman, Kyra Tuwaig, Erica Szwimer, Tal Zonshein, Gill Brody and Beth Doane. To the best family in the world: Rima, Mark, Steven, Sarah, Henry, Noah, Daniel, Zoe, Khiara, and Mom, Dad, Michelle and Bubby—thank you for all you do and all you are.